Walking In the Wilderness

Discovering the Attributes of God

By

Alice Steward

Unless otherwise specified, all Scripture quotations are taken from the King James Version.

Dedicated

To my Heavenly Father,
His Son and the Holy Spirit-
Who inspired the writing of "Walking in the Wilderness."
Also, to those who have a desire to understand the attributes of God

Acknowledgement

Many thanks for the support from my three daughters, Taunja Miles, Cornelia Runnels, and La'Donna White-Shirley, and Special thanks to my grandchildren for their constant love and support

Contributors.

1. Dr. Amanda Johnson Ogbonna (Book Editor)
2. Mr. Oladimeji Alaka (Book Cover Designer)

About the author

Alice Steward grew up in a dysfunctional family. At an early age, she received the call of God in her life. As an adult, she received the call to ministry. She continues to live a faithful Christian life to serve God in all parts of her life. God was not ready to send her into the mission field until there was preparation for her life to Evangelize. She has written a previous book, "Our Comfort Zone," for the church's edification. Its intention is to help bring in God's children before the end time. She's a follower of God and a true believer that God has chosen her to help with God's lost sheep. Alice Steward has received a Bachelor's degree in Theology from American Bible College in Oklahoma City, Ok. In May 1997.

About the book

This book uncovers some of the mysteries of God in the spiritual realm to help us gain a deeper understanding of God and His will and how he will mold us to become dedicated workers for Him. For us to achieve this, we must seek God daily in prayer, asking that we have spiritual ears and seeing eyes because prayer is vital to our Christian growth and maturity. God's Words reveal His will, and we must know it in order to pray effectively in agreement with it. God will begin to speak to us, for Jesus declared, *"My sheep hear my voice, and I know them, and they follow me"* (John 10:27). Just as sheep learn to recognize and obey their shepherd's voice, we must learn to become acquainted with His voice and His ways. Walking in the wilderness presents the insight and truth God has taught her through the ten years of wilderness travel.

Table of Contents

Introduction

As I journeyed through the wilderness, which lasted for ten years, I was not always as trusting in God as I am today. There were highs and lows in my life; I am only human with a sinful nature. For a while, at times, I was so depressed that I wondered if God had left me, even though I was trying to live a Christian life with Him. I surrendered my whole body and soul to His will. Even though Joshua 1:5 says that He will never fail us nor forsake us

I would become wrapped up in anger because I knew I was trusting in God, and problems were still arising. Trusting in Him but not enough; when things got hard, I deserted the ship. I became angry with God because I was doing everything He requested of me, and why were these things happening? I was still a babe in Christ, crying to my daddy to no avail. He wanted me to grow up so I could go about His business and help in the kingdom. He is a God who gave us our desires and feelings for us to control. He does not want us to be robots. As I waddled in pity, it got me nothing but a few steps backward from what He had called me to do. I knew He was saying within Himself, "Grow up!

Where can I find strength?

There were times I wanted to stop studying God's words, but when I did, a part of me was missing, and then I would go to God and apologize because of my bad behavior. Then I began to realize these things couldn't be coming from the Father. I am within His will, so I knew it was an attack from the enemy (Satan), wanting me to abandon the ship. As I continued to separate myself from as much of the world as possible, only God and my family were my support. In Galatians 1:17-19 After Paul's conversion experience with Jesus on Damascus Road, he did not go to Jerusalem to be with the other brothers and sisters but went to the Arabian desert to be taught by the Holy Spirit before entering into the church at Jerusalem.

Every day, I would meet God in prayer, and mostly, at the same time, the Holy Spirit would be there to give me support. My Bible says in John 16:7 that Jesus said, "I must go away so that the Holy Spirit would come and be our comforter, friend and guide." As I continued in God's words, my journey became a little smoother as long as I knew my Holy Spirit was there for me. I kept our friendship, communing with Him from when I opened my eyes to when I laid my head down on my pillow. Whenever a new day arose, before my feet touched the carpet, I would say to my friend, "Good morning, Holy Spirit." In my spirit, I would visualize him smiling at me. After I began to fellowship with the

Father's Spirit, I knew I would make it as long as I could have my comforter, my friend, and my guide. He would supply whatever I needed, not what I wanted but what I needed. He was there for me. I love Him so much, I cannot put it into words; there were times I would think about His goodness and cry tears of joy, which is something different for me. I had been accustomed to shedding tears from pain, not joy. There is pain and suffering in the wilderness. If you are willing to walk with Jesus, there is peace and joy in the pain and a learning experience to share with others to help bring them out with a testimony. There is light outside the wilderness when you come out with Jesus. If you ever need someone who will stick closer than a brother, invite Him into your life, and you will never regret it. I can't explain to you how you would need to try Him for yourself. If it was not for my Holy Spirit, I know, without a doubt, I would not have made it through the wilderness; it is a lonely journey that one should let the Father select for him/her.

Through God's words and my friends, when things became hard, I knew I was living according to God's law, keeping my body pure for God from sunrise to sunset. There was no need to blame God for my unhappiness. In the meantime, while I was praying and praying hard, keeping scriptures coming from my mouth, constantly shutting out any avenue that the devil could enter and what he has put in my mind, through prayer, it could not stay. It cannot cross the blood of Jesus. Amen! That was another way for me to learn scriptures, too! This was my greatest problem, thinking that if I were in the will of God, life would be a charm, but that is not true. We are going through this system that belongs to the enemy for now, and he will taunt us to try and turn us away from the plans of God for His children. So prepare yourself; there is no escaping problems. We will experience them and need to know how to go through them. God the Father is the way, the truth, and the life (John 14:6); there is no other way. After trials and staying in God's words, I began to join true forces with God against the tricks of the enemy, and I survived. Yes, I still have highs and lows, but I pray and believe in what I pray and doubt not. I pray myself out of it because I found out that God is "AWSOM." He has given us everything He has, which is His Son. And through Him, I can have what my heart desires and more if I pay the price—giving all I have to the Father, that is His anyway. To completely surrender wholeheartedly to the master is the price of submission.

The more we surrender our lives to the Father, the more He can use each and every one of us in every area of our lives so that we may become an asset to the kingdom. Jesus said, " a half-hearted commitment of those who say they would like to follow Him after they tended first to other duties: no man having put his hand to the plow, and looking back is fit for the kingdom of God (Luke 9:62).

These chapters are things I learned as I journeyed through the wilderness with my wonderful friend and companion who stuck closer than a brother. As you read from cover to end of this book, I hope God's grace and the Holy Spirit's leading will lead, guide, and open your spiritual eyes and both ears as mine were open. I love the Father because He does not hold a whip over us and drive us to do anything we do not want. We accept as he wills. Just a closer walk with Him, and everything will be all right. Try Him, and you will see.

The day is near, and destruction is close at hand. Don't procrastinate; there is no time. What He did for me, He will do the same for anyone else who surrenders completely to His will. The Father has no special sheep. He loves us all the same. He gives more to some and less to another. It is all about how much you give to Him; give, and you will receive.
For the battle is not yours but the Lords! (2Chronicles 20:15)
May God bless you in your walk with Him!

Chapter One

The Blood of Jesus

"Where will you spend eternity?" The first step to seeking eternal life is understanding the blood's purpose. The blood of Jesus is so important! Leviticus, which means the law of the Levites' was given to the Israelites during their journey in the wilderness. These laws were to keep their spiritual, moral, and physical purities. Every year, there was a ritual initiative by the high priest for the people using a scapegoat (a person or thing bearing blame for others). And this scapegoat was used for the removal of their sins. After the goat had been offered to God, the high priest laid his hand on the head of the goat and confessed the sins of the people; then, the goat was led away into the wilderness, which symbolized taking away the sins of the people.

We don't bring animal sacrifices as the Israelites needed to, but we must still have our sins atoned for by blood (Colossians 1:12-15). God, taking into consideration our infirmities, created a plan of salvation with better provision to save His children. He sent

His only begotten Son to die and shed His blood for the remission of our sins. Jesus's death appeased the anger of God against human wickedness, and we were delivered from the consequences of sin that is death (Romans 6:23). When you are cleansed with the blood of Jesus, everything is alright because there's nothing between you and God. He knows you are clean when your sins are forgiven, and you are in right standing with God and can fellowship with Him and other believers (1 John 7-9).

Sin is the failure to observe God's law. 1 John 1:9 says: *"If we confess our sins, He is faithful and just to forgive us our sins, and to cleanse us from all unrighteousness.* When we make a true confession to God for our sins, God completely separates sin from us. "Why spill the blood of goats or sheep? Jesus's blood was spilled for all. It is a lasting memorial for our sins. The blood is pure and cleanses us from our sins. Where there is liberty, there is freedom. Christ is the propitiation for our sins that covers them, and the Father will see them no more. There is power in the blood, supernatural power. It is a one-time acceptance of freedom from our sins that keeps us from dying, and for eternity. The Lord is our scapegoat; there is no need for any other.

God sent His only Son to save His children from bondage; love for us is the reason God was separated from His Son. Jesus paid the price that no one else could (1 Corinthians 6:19-20). If we accept Jesus as our Savior and continue to seek Him, we will have life, bringing a smile to His face because He sees that what He did for us was a worthwhile decision. As we walk in His counsel every day, He blesses us with our heart desires, and we continue to be sons and daughters of God the most high. There is power and strength in the blood just for the asking. There is nothing that the blood cannot do for us; even though we were once lost in our sins, God made provision for His children. He did not want His plans completely sabotaged by what Adam and Eve did when they were deceived by the tempter (Genesis 3: 1-24). Man was created for God's special use. He did not want us to perish. It wasn't our fault; it was a generational curse handed down to us, not for the asking. But the plans of God surpass that of the devil.

Grace is sufficient; where there is grace, there is liberty. It is there for our choosing. He gave us all our freedom of choice, so we choose where we will spend eternity. He is the most wonderful, loving Father that we have. Oh, how wonderful of a father we have. He cares for us. Jesus went through a separation for us; how much more He would do for us; it is there for the asking. "Oh, come" to Jesus right now! And ask for it; all you have to do is open your mouth and say the word. "Come to Jesus, and He will accept you and cover your sins forever. There is nothing you have done in the past in your life that the blood will not cover. Come to Him, my children, and let Him take you into His bosom. Let Him love you and give you safety from the tricks of the evil one.

Life here may be rough, but this is not our final stop. *"He said come to me all ye that are laden I will give you rest (Matthew 11:28). He is talking to us.* There is no other way to receive eternal rest but in the blood of Jesus. Life might have been unfair; there is nothing you can do about that, but here is an opportunity to start all over again the right way.

So don't wait for tomorrow, for there might not be a tomorrow. "Come to Jesus right now." The Bible said, "Don't put off for tomorrow what you can do today; no man knows the day or hour (Matthew 24:36). So do it right now and seek peace right now. "Where will you spend eternity? That is the question to put in your heart: where will you spend eternity? Only you can answer that question.

Chapter Two

The living water; A thirst and hunger for righteousness

John 4: 1-42: On the way to Galilee, Jesus went through Samaria. At Sychar, He then rested by the well while His disciples went to buy food. A woman came to draw water. When Jesus asked her for a drink, she was startled, for Jews had no dealing with Samaritans. When He told her of her past life, she knew that He was a prophet, and Jesus confessed to her that He was the Messiah. The woman left her water pot, ran to the city, and told the town folk that she had found the Messiah. So the people left the city and went out to Him; many at once believed in Him and begged Him to stay. For two days, He taught them; then they said: "This is truly the Christ, the Savior of the world!" (Kirby.30)

The woman at the well, yes, was a Samaritan woman who was thirsty, not only for water but for the spirit of God. She came to draw water, and she got the living water, where she would never thirst again. She didn't know about Jesus like some of us; we need

Him, but we are not seeking Him. And when we find Him, we don't accept Him. He is looking and waiting for us to receive him in our everyday walk. This will give us eternal life. The gift that the Father is willing to give. Freely He gives, freely we should receive. You don't pay any money, but there is a price, the price of obedience. What do you have to lose? Take Him now and see what the Lord will do for you. She didn't expect what she received; she started running everywhere, telling everyone she saw about the living water she found and that she didn't have to pay any money; it is free for the choosing. "O taste and see.

"O children, He is calling you softly and gently, "O taste and see what is freely given to you. He is sweet, gentle, and waiting to carry you home to the Father. Harden not your heart in the time of provocation (Hebrews 3:8). "Let not your heart be troubled, if you believe in the Father you will believe in me (John 14: 1). It is time to come running to the living water the Father has sent to you. "Come and see what He has sent to you; it is free for the asking. O my children, time is running out; Jesus said, "I am waiting to carry you through just for the asking." Life is short, so come to Him right now. He is waiting to carry you home; the enemy is waiting, too. Choose ye today whom you will serve; the choice is yours.

Jesus said, "I am the way, the truth, and the life; no man may come to the Father except through me" (John 14: 6). Come, O come, the days are short and the nights are long. Jesus is saying, "I am here to carry you home. Don't wait!" Please don't wait there is no reason to wait. Procrastinating is a dangerous thing to do. The water is freely given unto all who are thirsty. Do like the women at the well; come and find out about the special water you can receive. Jesus is calling in all His sheep by name. He knows His sheep and calls them by name. They were given to Him when He shed His blood for the world. He paid the price no man could. He is very special to all who call upon his name and enter that special covenant with Him. You will get your clothes rinsed and cleaned with the purifying blood of Jesus.

Once you are free from sin, you will never want to go back into bondage if you are truly free. When you find green pasture, you will want to enjoy it and lie around heaven all day.

A gift from God

Saint of God, get ready to enjoy what you have never experienced before; you will never have to give it up after you enter. Try it out and see what God has for you. This is an opportunity you may never get again. Come to Jesus right now. Come "O come" be like the women at the well. Be full, and you will never want again. There is joy and peace in the water, not something to wet your lips. The water will carry you home. To be in want is not too good, but having your desired fulfilment is wonderful; you don't know what you are missing if you don't come and see. The offer today is still standing, so reach out and touch the hem of His garment and get your issues healed (Mark 5: 21-43).

A crowd of people gathered around Jesus, and one woman, who had spent all she had on doctors without being cured, came behind and touched the edge of His robe; " For she said, *"if I but touch His garment, I shall be well."* Jesus turned at once, saying: *"Who touched me?"* The woman, trembling, confessed. "*Daughter, your faith has healed you." Jesus said, "Go in peace"*. There is not one issue He will heal; there are a multitude of them.

He is the rock and shield of our salvation; He is our Elshaddai. He is our consuming fire that will consume you and clean you like silver and gold just for the asking. We need Him, "O how we need Him. "O come and see" what God has provided for His faithful children. Everyone will not taste of this water, only a few ones, not by His choosing but by the ones seeking to be filled with the living water Jesus is offering. Don't let your heart be troubled; if you believe in Jesus, You will receive if you seek.

Knock, and the door of grace will open, and you may come in. The bath water is cool and will have a lot of effects on your body, and so is the living water of God, but this will affect you forever. This is the time, Saints of God when the water is freely given, and you can freely receive it here for the asking. Choices are free; also, you will not be pushed into the spring of life. It flows from here to Calvary, which is rich with the blood of Jesus: "O come and see what God has given His precious sheep. He loves us all. He is our Shepherd. In the provisions of God, there are no strings attached; there is only complete submission to the laws and ways of God. There is no other way. He is our shield and rock. In Psalm 18:2, David said, *"The Lord is my rock, and my fortress, and my deliverer; my God, my strength in whom I will trust; my buckler, and the horn of my salvation, and my tower.* In Psalm 33:20, he said, *"Our soul waited for the Lord: He is our help and our shield.*" Just for the asking, pray to the Master, and He will give you the strength to come and pick up our beds and follow Him to the well of cool, fresh water.

After you drink, you will never thirst again; "That's what I am talking about" Hallelujah! I don't want to keep running and falling, trying to get full over and over. I want to be filled and stay that way. I would like for my body to continue to rejoice in God. No more pain and no more sorrow is what God has for His covenant children; it's just there for the asking. "O come and see" what the Lord has for His covenant children. Anyone will not receive of this water; it is a special water that will fill you, and you will never want again. You won't have to keep running, asking for the water Jesus has for us. "There is something about the man Jesus, He is AWESOME."

When He was crucified on the cross, and they pierced His side, that was the living water that He had to offer them, and it was spilled on the ground, last chance, and you know they lost out. We all know what happened to the men who crucified our Savior, lost in perdition. Some of them probably wish they could have gone against the order of Pilate during Jesus's crucifixion and asked Jesus, "Please give me what you gave the women at the well," and He would have said to them, "You good and faithful servant, I will see that one day I will meet you in paradise." He would have come down from that cross and kissed all that believed, even the king. That is the kind of savior we have, a compassionate one. He loves us all. He gave His life for many who will receive the water He has to give. Jesus is the way, truth, and the life. Come to Him today before it's too late. Jesus is waiting; the door to salvation is still open.

They will be closing after Christ has received all that God had given Him to find rest in the flowing water of Jesus. "Water, Water, Water! The precious pure water!

"I am going to keep the water the Lord gave me, Amen!" Continually let it flow from me to as many as God appoints for me to share the words of life and lead them to the fountain that flows with that living water. You don't know what you are missing until you try Jesus!

He is the rock to build your home on a true, solid foundation that will not shift or turn. You can be sure of standing on Him and will not fall. If you stumble, He will help you get back up; there is no need to try on your own. He is here; call on Him and ask Jesus to give you the same water He freely gave the Samaritan women who had five husbands, none of which was her own. Amen!

If He did it for her, He will do it for anyone. The Samaritans were not people that the Jews would waste their time on, but Jesus did. He is willing to give everyone the water of life, and when we start running to tell others about that water Jesus has given us, He will be in heaven shouting all over heaven. He does not want any of us to perish but come to repentance and live.

He is not a partial God; He will do the same for drunks, drug addicts, and whatever addiction you may be hiding in the closet. He will air out your dirty laundry if you will come to Him with a willing heart. Come to Jesus the way you are; don't try to wash your own clothes; you don't have the cleaning solution that he has. Come and see what the Lord can do for you and I. Amen.

Chapter Three

Anointing of God

When one does not honor one's position in God, He will choose one that will. God sent the Prophet Samuel to the house of Jesse to anoint David out of the house of Jesse. One who was after the heart of God! The anointing in his life made him different from the other chosen king. He fell and stumbled but asked forgiveness and didn't completely fall by the way side because God was there to hear his cry.

He reigned in victory over Israel for forty years, fearing God all the way. He was the greatest King in the history of Israel. In Psalm 23, David said, *"God has prepared a table before me in the presence of my enemies, he anointed my head with oil my cup runneth over. Surely goodness and mercy shall follow me all the days of my life. And I will dwell in the house of the Lord forever."* David knew whatever difficulties he faced with the anointing of God, he would be delivered. And he would worship God all the days of his life.

Supernatural, the anointing of God on one's life is like oil poured over your head, which runs over your body—giving you the strength to accomplish whatever responsibility you have been placed in. The anointing is the power of God that he has given each and every one of us to stand in the office He has assigned us; it is the power to respond, the power to act, the power to supersede that of a normal person (Judges 3-16). "Sampson, one of the judges of Israel, exhibits supernatural strength at various times. It was not of human strength because the Spirit of the Lord came upon him to accomplish great deeds. Once with a jawbone of an ass, he killed one thousand men. At his death, he was given strength by God to slew three thousand people; the Bible said he slew at his death more than he had in his life; that is the power of God being displayed in the strength of man.

The ability of God is the power that comes into action in one's life; it is not of ourselves but God. You no longer work on the authority of man but of God. The anointing is the power one needs to excel above anything possible. You can recognize it because it shows beyond anything that we can achieve on our own. God is the one who passes this into our lives. There is nothing we can do to provoke this. God gives this power to those He has chosen to perform what He has called them to do. And to accomplish what He has called them to perform without any hardship placed on the individual. In Psalms 23:5, *"When David said my cup runneth over with oil,"* he was speaking about God's favor through God's strength, through which he performed everything God placed upon his life to handle, to deliver, to conquer, to pursue. David knew that whatever difficulties he faced, with God's anointing, he would be delivered. And he would worship God all the days of his life. The anointing of God manifests in you when there is a special call on your life to perform the duties of God.

He is not a God who calls you and puts you on the frontline without your armor. He gives us what we need. God desires us to do everything He has called us into in an orderly way so that it will be done decently and in order (1 Corinthians 14:40). Don't go out on your own; you might fail. But to go out commissioned by the Lord, you will supersede your call. You will receive the Strength of the Lord, which the impossible will be upon your life. You are no longer in self but in God. The mind is a terrible thing to loose trying to figure out the things of God; let Him control your ability, and He will greatly set you upon higher places that you may have never arrived at.

Complete Submissiveness

God is waiting to use us, but you will have to completely surrender your body and soul to God so that the supernatural oil of God will empower you to do the supernatural things of God. Strength and power from God is awesome! When it shows up, you will know it is something no one can fake. That is the only way we, as humans, can assume that type of strength. It is not our strength but God's strength to accomplish His calling on our lives. Everyone that God has called can receive the anointing, but there is a price you have to pay. It is freely given if you pay the price. "It is not money!

The anointing is the oil that flows over our life when we can stand before God and man and say here I am, use me, "Praise God! God is willing to share it with His servants out of obedience. The anointing of God is what we all should desire, as a very pleasing and satisfying ministry to God and yourself. You cannot claim your accomplishment on self but on God. Everyone will know you have it by what you say and do. It is visible without trying to tell everyone you have it. It is like a light that shines on your life and will open doors that you can't or could not have opened. So, if you want your light to shine before man and God, you have to be obedient to receive this gift before God. This is a wonderful accomplishment to have. There is no need to pray for it without the obedience of God. You will not deserve it and will not receive it. Praying and fasting will help, but there is a part of being cleansed and free of impurities that the body has to stop the flow. In Psalms 51:10-11, David said, *"Create in me a clean heart, O'*

God; and renew a right spirit within me. Cast me not away from thy presence, and take not thy Holy Spirit from me." That is why when David sinned against God's law, he asked God not to take the anointing away from him. He did not want the presence of God and all His provision to depart from him; he would be on his own. He prayed that God would continue to dwell with him and give him the heart that he needed to accomplish the things of God. The anointing does not continue to exist in a body that is not pure.

Anointing of the body and mind is what we need to become supernatural beings of God in the flesh. Anointing on one's life can break the yoke of whatever bondage you may enter. The chains will drop to the ground; all you will have to do is step out and walk straight without that handicap. God wants to use each and every one of us so that we can walk out in faith with the confidence that we will accomplish this, do it right, and be proud of our calling. He will not leave us or forsake us (Psalms 27:9). He will be there to carry us through so we may accomplish what He has prepared us to do. Amen! Anointing of God is wonderful; it is refreshing to know that you walk with God, and it is pleasing to God, too! That is all He wants is for each and every one of us: to walk with Him. God will hold your hand and direct you on the right path; you won't fall if you do. He is willing to pick you up before you hit the ground. It is not His desire for us to stumble or fall but to accomplish the things we have been called to do.

The anointing of God is the Spirit of God, and it is wonderful and so sweet to have. You will never be the same. Amen! Hallelujah, praise God.

"I love the Father. He is so good to each and every one of us; all His provisions are to ensure our job is performed in the uttermost strength of God." *The* anointing of God is the strength of God, not our strength but His strength. The anointing of God gives us the favor of God, too, to reward us for our obedience to Him. Out of obedience, God will give us almost anything our hearts desire; there is a price to pay. Jesus paid one for us when He bled and died for our sins; it is free and worth having. We can follow the example of Christ and keep our eyes on His accomplishment for us, and what we do can and will not ever compare to what He did for God's covenant children. So, if you want the anointing light of God to shine on your life, you will have to become completely submissive to God's whole heart and soul, and He will take you places that you have not been before. I can't tell you when, and I can't tell you where this will happen in your life. All I can say is to get ready and stay that way. You can't fool Him; He knows your heart. Ask for a pure heart like David, and that will get you where you have never been before. If we could ask a few of the chosen ones of the Bible about the goodness of God, they would testify they have served God and are now in His bosom, resting for the final time when God will raise them to life again. I am sure they are resting in peace because the anointing of God will give you that peace. After all, you will be sure to rise again at the appointed time.

When the Spirit of God is in control of a person's heart, blessing and success are the result, but when selfish desires are in control, it results in punishment and failure.

Losing the anointing

Saul, the king of Israel, was the son of Kish, a Benjamite; He was anointed king by Samuel the prophet. He disobeyed God and was rejected by Him. He was so jealous of David's popularity with the people that he sought to kill Him. When the anointing of God departed from him, he went into battle without the anointing and never returned. While in battle, he was wounded. Afraid of being captured alive, he ended his own life (1 Samuel). Losing the anointing for us may not be as drastic as that of Saul, who knew the consequence. Any hardship in our lives will become a sore spot that no one will want to wait for the healing. Take the example of Saul and many others in biblical times: stay under the anointing of the most high God, and we can be sure to receive blessings and not curses.

To recognize the infilling of the Spirit

The infilling of the Holy Spirit is a transformation of the *body* and mind. Once we think for ourselves, now we have spiritual help. We will know Him because our thoughts will become God's thoughts, leading us to do the things of God. It is a new format kind of thinking. Your spirit will intertwine as a matter of thinking with the thinking of the most high. This infilling of the spirit will cause us to do what God has intended for us to accomplish; our purpose in life has been the order of the Lord. The infilling of the Holy Spirit is a fresh anointing on us, giving us the knowledge we would not have if we were thinking on our own. It is supernatural; it's the power of God that dwelled in the new temple of God. We will know when we have it because of a new, fresh thinking that comes from within. The infilling of the Holy Spirit comes from above; you cannot obtain this on your own. Prayer is a part of obtaining this, but there are other things we have to do to be able to wear this special mantle. The infilling of the Holy Spirit is wonderful, and you will begin to want to share the knowledge of God with everyone you see.

It is the mantle of God that wraps you tight and keeps you secure for His purpose; it is an awesome experience you will never want to lose. That's why Saul was so upset with David when he thought God had left him. He would become a man like everyone else. Yes, he was a king, but he did not have the power and authority that God had passed upon him. The infilling of the Holy Spirit is a cloak and dagger that pierces our inner being and keeps us; no one can touch this because it is of God. Only we can make this depart from us. The infilling of the Holy Spirit is sweet and a wonderful thing to have. It will bring out abilities within us that we never ever thought we possessed. Some of the most genius people on earth have been wrapped with the infilling, and some wonder how they were so gifted in having natural mental abilities to develop their ideas. Get the complete infilling of God's Spirit, and you will see.

It changes you in and out; it is nothing that you or I should be jealous of. God is the giver of His Spirit. It's a supernatural power that is put within us for whatever reason God's purpose is. Again, it is a part of how you surrender to God. You take your thoughts and soul and surrender all you have to God. That will open great doors for you; if you want to move God, that is the key that you will use to pursue after God's heart, and He will intertwine, and you will become one with God. I am speaking about the supernatural on a spiritual plane, which is not an earthly thing. An infilling is still active today because God lives in every one of us and is willing to enter and become one. He is not a God that does favor; you earn what He does for you. What you want from God, you give, and He will give. It is the same with our tithes! He has enough of His Spirit to give to as many as would like to receive. The infilling started in the Old Testament, was prophesied into the new, and is active in our generation. It is here to give us the power to perform what we have been called to do. God will give every one of us the tools to build whatever we desire for a small price, which we can give without any hardship on you or me. I am not speaking about the impossible. What He has done for one is available for everyone who believes. "People, I am not speaking about earthly things that man has designed, but the invention of God."

Man's invention has a chance of falling apart, but God's creation is here to stay. We are supposed to last, but the trickster was the cause of the fall. God has many other plans for us to make up for what has happened. He will not sit around and cry about what has changed His plans; it was taken out of His hands. God is so cleaver He will take another route to alleviate the situation. So that everything He has for us, we will still accomplish through the intervention of God. Amen! Listen, this power is waiting for all, not a few. Look, and you will see a new man surface; you will look almost the same, but you will not be the same; you will become a lovely creation of God, made in His image to carry out His plans, and will succeed because of the infilling of the Holy Spirit. You won't fail if you forsake self and let God master your life. It's not geared toward a robot experience but a spiritual endeavor. The wrapping of God's Spirit over your spirit is a spiritual encounter; maybe everyone will not be able to comprehend or believe, but I tell you, it is here for us all. Amen!

When you hear about having a supernatural charge, this is similar to the ever-ready rabbit that keeps on going and going and will have nothing on you. We will go! Go! And go! Only God will stop this flow. So let's get up and try God, get the infilling of the Holy Spirit. He is standing at the door of your heart, waiting to come in. knock! Knock! Can't you hear him? That was just a little humor to help you know there is still fun and jokes; there is humor and joy in the things of God. He can't use robots. He wants his children to enjoy what He has for us to the fullest. It is our fault if we don't receive it. When Jesus said in Matthew 7:7, "To ask and you will receive" what*? What your heart desires!*
I don't know what that is. Ask Him and see the impossible happen in your life.

That is what the infilling of the Holy Spirit is to us: a taste of the supernatural charge of God. It is of our generation and will not go anywhere because God is still alive within all His covenant children. Have you checked your heart lately? If it is still beating, then you know that God is alive. When God breathes, we breathe; when He walks, we walk with Him. If He dies, we will die; we are made in the image of God and the sheep of His pasture. "It is the most wonderful news I have ever heard." What a powerful thing God did for us, his children.

He always has us in mind. That's one of the reasons Jesus died for us, so we could enjoy the plans God wants to share with His children. Now, let's not sit around depressed about what we don't or can't have; we should seek God's things, and I know He will show up! I don't know when, and I don't know how! I guarantee you He will show up! You might even be asleep, and He comes to you and says wake up, real gentle; here is a task for you to handle today. And it will be so awesome you will say, "Awe, man! That awesome God is speaking to me, Oh! I must be truly loved by God! With each encounter, you will become more and more attaché to the spirit of God, possessing the wiliness to be available to serve at all times. You will never want to be detached and lose what you have desired for so long and really, with some doubt, didn't believe. Get on the bandwagon and ride with God. The infilling of the Holy Spirit is a supernatural being that lives within us, giving us some of the attributes of God. I said some, not all. There is only one God, and there will never be another; you cannot duplicate Him. Being gods, we need power in our lives. What better way to receive it than the infilling of the Holy Spirit?

Lives will change for the best; it will be all about God and not ourselves. It won't be a hardship for us because the things of God will be our desire and won't be something that we will be forced into. After receiving the infilling of the Holy Spirit, please don't become like King Saul in 1Samuel 1-19; when the Spirit of God departed from him, he became bitter and had a murdering spirit because he knew that all the power that God had given him was taken away and now he was an ordinary man with only Kingship authority not godly. He became somewhat confused because his thinking was of human nature and not the supernatural thinking of God. There is a great difference between being stripped of your rank in God's anointing. "I would assume that the reason he wanted David around was not to play his harp but to see if David had received what he had lost from God. Take the lesson from Saul: Keep what God has given you and do right with it, and you won't have to become bitter about what you once had, which has been taken away and given to someone more deserving. It was the same with the talents; the one who has was given, the one who had the lazy one, it was taken away (Matthews 25:14-30). It is a lesson in all that life has for us, especially God's things. Seek to learn, and you will grow, either in wisdom and knowledge of God or the garbage of the world. The infilling of the Holy Spirit is what will take a simple shepherd boy and make him into a king over his people. That is what is spoken of as one of the impossible of God. What we cannot do for ourselves, we have a very loving and caring Father who is able, willing, and ready to do the supernatural in our lives.

"As I write this book, the Spirit of the Lord is touching my inner being and teaching me about the things of God and how we, as God's children, can do all things in Christ who strengthens us (Philippians 4:13). He is the God of the impossible! It might be impossible with man but not with God (Luke 1:37). That is a powerful statement! If you can believe, you will receive. God is a transformer of one's life; your faith is what activates this through His Spirit. The more faith, the more you become transformed. In everything of God, you cannot get around that word faith! That is the wind that turns the wheel of destiny into what you want God to perform in your life. Faith combines with the Spirit of God; what an awesome team, the Indwelling of the Holy Spirit resting in us. There are times when you may wonder what to do. He will speak to you, maybe about your life or the things of God. He will lead you, tell you how to solve the problem in question, and tell you about the awesome things of God that man cannot reveal because He is God. He shared with us His nature, and with that, He will keep us on the right path in the will of God. We will not go into anything with closed eyes. He is the keeper of one's soul and mind. He is the key to happiness and love for every one of His children. There is so much to speak about God's Spirit. I don't think one person knows enough to write it down or to speak, but I do know He lives within my soul, and I love Him for who He is and what He is to me. "Hallelujah!! That's the supernatural work of God. "He Is God!!

Chapter four

"Angels"

Dedicated to the late Reverend Jeanette Murphy

Works of the ministering spirits:

What are ministering spirits? Angels are messengers, supernatural or heavenly beings; they are a little higher in dignity than man (Psalms 8:5). God commanded the creation of angels, and they were created. He set them in place forever, and that decree will never become void. "God said by faith the world was created at His command, that what is seen was not made out of what was visible. He spoke things into existence. Angels were here before the creation of man. They are described as "spirit. They are not flesh, but sometimes they have revealed themselves in bodily form to man. They do not marry or die. They are stronger than men; they are not omnipotent or omniscient like God.

Angels have different ranks and different gifts; angels were created holy. Some fell from their state of innocence (2 Peter 2:4). Their fall occurred before the fall of man, for Satan to deceive

Eve in the garden of Eden. Their work varied; good angels stand in the presence of God and worship Him (Matthews 18:10). Their position to His children is to protect and deliver them. They have an important place in the life and ministry of Christ. They made an appearance in the birth of Jesus and the shepherds. After the wilderness temptation of Christ, they ministered to Him (Matthews 4:11). An angel strengthened Him in the garden (Luke 22:43). An angel rolled away the stone from the tomb (Matthews 28:2-7). Angels were with Him at the ascension. Scripture shows that good angels will continue in the service of God. The evil angels will have their place in the lake of fire with Satan (Matthews 25:41).

Provisions of God

Psalms 91:11-14 says: "For He shall give His angels charge over thee, to keep thee in all thy ways. They shall bear thee up in their hands, lest thou dash thy foot against a stone. Thou shall tread upon the lion and adder: the young lion and the dragon shalt thou trample under feet. Because he hath set His love upon me therefore will I deliver him: I will set him on high, because he hath known my name! He will command his angel concerning us to guard us in all our ways.

When trouble arises, when we have no control, God will send His force in to take over; the only thing we have to do is keep faith and remember the covenant of God. He said He would be with us in trouble, deliver us with honor and long life, satisfy us, and show us His salvation provision. Angels are manifested by God to serve the universe as He sees necessary. They are the army of God. At His command, they are ready to join forces against the enemy. God created them for our protection and to help guide His people. Angels are our servants to use according to God's word, not for our selfish use. They are not like the fallen angels of Satan; they are the ones who are here to help us fall into temptation and to separate us from the plans of God.

When Christ was in the garden of Gethsemane, He said, "I give up my life; no man can take it." He could have had legions of angels to wage war against the enemy and won. They are more mighty than men. Angels are the eyes of our protection. When danger arises, God disperses them to protect us from the enemy, something we cannot do; they disperse as many as God sees necessary to handle the job. No weapon formed against us shall prosper (Isaiah 54:17). Angels are the task force of God, willing to aid Him whenever he calls. They are obedient and love God and the plans of God.

They are the ones who will help separate the sheep from the goats, or better yet, the good from the evil, another step closer to God's people from Satan's people. They come in ranks, with duties given to them, as we are also to follow commands from

God. Whatever the command of God is, they will carry it out. They have a mind and will of their own; that is the reason when Satan fell, he carried one-third of the angel down from heaven with him. When God created heaven and earth, He was very considerate in giving each of us our own minds to do what we like. He didn't want robots running around in heaven and earth. We are agents of free will, and that pleases God. It puts a smile on His face, just knowing when we serve Him, it is out of love.

In so many ways, angels are little children like us but are mighty; their jobs call for supernatural strength. Have you ever thought about Moses as he stood upon the rock with a staff in his hands, and God told him to point it toward the red sea, and it opened? It was not Moses; God sent many angels to perform that duty, and it was supernatural. They are supernatural beings, special in so many ways; God created them that way. His plans are not for us to understand but to take full advantage of His provisions.

God loves us so much we cannot count His provision for us; what more can He do to prove His love for us? His plans are always through, no part missing, no part broken. He is the master of the universe. You can see that by the creation, no ordinary person or idol could have done this. He is real, and He will live in every one of us if we let Him.

When David threw that small stone from the sling, it was David's faith that caused the supernatural work of the angel to knock Goliath down in victory, not the stone, another victory of God through the faith of man. So, by knowing that, if we have faith, God will put it into action. Our faith is the wheel that drives the action of God. There are times when angels manifest in human form because there is something God wants us to know. If they are in angelic form, we can't hear or see them. They are continually serving God and us. No command other than those that agree with the plans of God will they obey.

Kathryn Kuhlman's main teaching theme was miracles; she would say, "I believe in miracles, opening up doors to our understanding that they exist; maybe she had an encounter to make her understand they are a part of God's plans. If we are not taught about the plans of God, then how would we find out what He has for us to make our lives much easier? Without the supernatural forces of God, we would not be able to stand; eventually, we would be destroyed by fallen angels. They are not aggressive toward us because they know we are not by our self. They are fallen angels, but God was so good. He did not take their abilities away from them; they would receive their punishment in due time. We will all one day have to stand before God, the good and evil.

For us to serve God, we must be at peace with ourselves and the world. Our minds have to be clear to react to the words of God. If we are running around with fear and the cares of the world, we won't be able to serve Him, so He provided everything we needed to accomplish this. He said, "Peace I give you, not as the world gives" (John 14:27). If we are to enjoy the fruit of the spirit, we will have to have a mind that is at peace with all things. The battle is not ours but the Lord's (Isaiah 54:17). He has equipped every one of us to obtain victory in His name, and we can count on that.

If God wanted to use those angels He has by his side, He could tell them to slaughter all that do not believe, and it would be over, but our Father is so loving He gives us all an opportunity to come to repentance and be saved.

"I believe in miracles, too! I have had many encounters with angels, I believe in angels, and I thank God for angels. I give my angels command, and they follow it. I keep communication open with my angels every day. We don't have a causal conversation, but I give my angels commands and thank them for a job well done. I believe in angels, and so should you. Use what God has given us. It's there for the asking; they are waiting to serve us. Why not enjoy the luxury from the Lord? I truly believe in angels.

I had an unsightly old shed about to fall by my back door. My children and I took it apart board by board until it was ready to be carried away. Something happened while we were in the process of taking it apart that could have crushed me and our pet dog if it wasn't for the grace of God. Relatively speaking, we all could have died. We didn't know what we were doing and went about it the wrong way, knocking the building down by the post that held it up. The building was about to fall, and we didn't realize it wasn't going to fall the way we had intended. We heard a cracking sound, and it almost instantly began to collapse on us (my daughters Taunja, Connie, Peach, grandson Kelvin and Stevie, granddaughter Tani, me, and our pet dog). My daughters and grandchildren moved quickly. I tried to run and fell. To this day, I can feel the hands of angels pulling me to safety. My feet were a couple of inches away from destruction. God saved me and my dog! We made it, but I don't ever want that job again! I thank God for my ministering spirits! God gave us all angels to assist, protect, and deliver us. They protect us while we are asleep; we are never without protection, and we should always remember to utilize the provision of God.

If we continue to trust God in whatever situation we may be in, he will take charge of our lives and deliver us from any situation; nothing is impossible to those who believe.

David said in Psalm: *'I sought the Lord, and He answered me; he delivered me from all my fears.* And he said, "the angel of the Lord encamps around those who fear him, and he delivers them." And he said, "taste and see that the Lord is good; blessed is the man who takes refuge in him."

Chapter five

Disobedient To God

Being disobedient to God, you will be thrown into the lake of fire with Satan and his demons at the final time of separation. Disobedience is an abomination to God and His laws. God is a good and loving Father whose laws are fair and just. Grace is sufficient; where there is grace, there is freedom of choice. God is supreme over the world; what He asks of us is fair and just. There are rules for everyone. If you have a job, there are rules to follow, and we follow them in order to keep our position, so follow God's and keep your life. Man's rules are temporal, but God's are everlasting.

In the beginning, Adam and Eve had grace, but they took it upon themselves to abuse the grace of God and were tempted by other promises, which caused their disobedience. God could have stopped them, but He gave them His laws to follow, which was their decision. He is not our babysitter. God looks upon us with grace and mercy, giving us the time and space to live a productive life. If we choose a destructive life, we will end up in the same pit that Satan and his demonic angels will be thrown into; the choice is ours. Look at the situation and decide where you will spend eternity. Will it be in love and grace or in the lake of fire? Matthews 7:14 said, *"strait is the gate, and narrow is the way, which lead unto life, and few there be that find it."* The road is narrow, and few will find it; wide is the road, and many will see it. Find the right road and hop on it so that you will find the everlasting provision of God and experience something that earth has never provided; you won't experience this unless you earn it. Only you can make the decision; God will not disrupt your choice. Man was made for God, and God for man. He did not want this to happen to us; it was not in His plans, but He provided an escape for those of us who got caught up in the devil's schemes. It was a generational curse, but God created a new plan for those who inherited it. Galatians 3:13 said; *Christ hath redeemed us from the curse of the law, being made a curse for us: For it is written, cursed is everyone that hanged on a tree:* God needed to change the route of our inheritance; we can receive it if we trust in God and do the things of God, not the thing of the enemy. Time is short, so we need to decide what we want, to live or die. It is up to us to decide that! God does not have a list with any of His children listed on it for the lake of fire. That is why the world is still running its course, to give us ample time to get ready and stay that way because no man knows the day or hour when our savior will return. (Matthews 24:36) So get ready and stay that way. There is no time to procrastinate. Get ready, saints of God, and find what you didn't accomplish here on the earth.

This is not our final stop! There is another one waiting not for everyone, but the obedient ones of God. We should enjoy what God intended for us in the beginning before the plans are spoiled by someone who wants to be god.

Satan is a trickster; he will do anything to put you on the wrong side of the road. Make you promise that he will not keep, some he cannot even remember. He is a fake god with no intention or ability to save us. He knows he is destroyed without a doubt, so his evil plans are to take as many of God's children with him. He will do anything to destroy what God has planned for His children. There is no turning back for him. His time is on the clock, ticking down to his final day. He is laughing at us because he has deceived us into thinking that God is hard to deal with and that His laws are hard on our lives. Poverty, sickness, and disease are what Satan has to offer us; we have a choice: the love and provision of God or the destructed demise of the devil. He really is our enemy disguised as a friend. (Matthews 7:15) beware of ravenous wolves dressed in sheep clothing, with a smile on his face. He is the chief of fake gods with no power against the big God of the universe. So, we need to join forces with a winner or with a loser. "I want to enjoy the best of what God has; what about you? Amen!

Watch and Pray

In the final days, we don't know what it will be like; I don't want to find out. The Bible speaks about the gnashing of teeth and the streets filled with blood; it sounds pretty scary to me. I have experienced enough here on this earth instead of going into this and having a choice for peace. I would love to live in peace. I see here on earth that drinking, partying, and taking drugs to get high can lead you to destruction, and it also takes your youth and life away. This is not the provision of God; this is death the first time; you are waiting for the last. It will be more terrible than the first. God said it, and I believe it. He is not a God that lies (Numbers 23: 19). He gave us the Bible so we can see the experiences of those who disobey His laws, not to scare us, but for us to make a decision that is not what we want.

We want the fruit of the spirit (Galatians 5:22, 23; Love, joy, and peace). We want to lie in the bosom of our Father, where there is only happiness, not destruction. He also shows us in His word what good and wonderful things He will do to those who love Him and seek His face daily, not when we have a petition, but always. Matthews 6:33 said, *But seek ye first the kingdom of God, and His righteousness; and all these things shall be added unto you.* For He is not a God that He shall, nor want to lie! He is a God of truth. He said know the truth, and it will set you free. That sounds like good news. Hallelujah; Praise God. That kind of talking makes me happy! I am for what God wants because I know He is thinking about our destiny. So don't wait for tomorrow; it may never come. Prepare now and stay prepared, and we won't have to be concerned about the day of His coming; the Bible says He will come as a thief in the night, so we need to stay ready at all times. Thief means He will come suddenly without any warning. Stay ready, stay prepared, and you won't have to be concerned with that.

No man knows the day of His coming. I don't care how. Man, try and figure out his coming and never get it right. If they stay awake and pray, they won't have to figure that out. If your heart is not ready, you will miss the boat; the final choosing will come from the heart, which you cannot disguise. In Psalms 51:10, David said, *"Create in me a clean heart, O' God; and renew a right spirit within me."* David was after the heart of God, and he captured it. So if we pattern our life after David, we won't have to be concerned about the day or hour our Lord will return. The Bible says in Matthews 26:41: *"watch and pray that ye enter not into temptation: the spirit indeed is willing, but the flesh is weak.* God doesn't expect us to be perfect. We lost perfection in the garden of Eden, but there are things that separate us from the ungodly. If we draw near to

God and accept his plans of salvation, our hearts will let us know when we are doing something to defile the laws of our God.

Pray throughout the day, not when you have designated a time, but all the time. Keep God on your mind and His plans of salvation, and there will be no room for the enemy to come in. The biggest thing he will use on us is what we don't have and what we need. And God has promised to supply our needs. Tell the devil to get out of your business and plead the blood of Jesus over him, telling him you know you're a covenant child of God and no weapon form against you shall prosper (Isaiah 54:17). He will tuck tail and run and run fast. He is not going to argue with you when he sees that your mind is on God. He only lies around with the ones he can sleep with, buddy up with, feeding them all that crap about the prejudice of God, and that he has favorites, so do he. If you look at the situation, what is he talking about? He needs to put the shoes on the right foot and wear them himself; if they don't fit, pull them off and put them on who they belong to.

Don't listen to him; he will steal your life. Roman 8:35 says*:* *"who shall separate us from the love of Christ? Shall tribulation, or distress, or persecution, or famine, or nakedness, or peril, or sword?* Nothing should be able to separate us from the love of God. So please, we should be sure of whose voice we hear. Things of God are the best things to keep your mind full. Meditation on scripture and phrases of

God every day, trying to keep it fresh so there will be no room in our mind for the enemy. That's the reason we should meditate, to keep God on our mind, repeating over and over, to see if we still remember it. That's a good blockage of the mind against the deceit of the enemy.

Keep your guard up at all times, and don't forget because Satan won't. As soon as we forget, you will be able to tell you will start getting depressed, so when this happens, put the things of God right back into your thought, and everything will be all right; you'll be back on the right track. God's children have a tremendous amount of help. Call on your help, use what God has given us, and our walk with God won't be so hard. John 14:16 speaks about sending us a comforter, which is the Holy Spirit, who will provide us help, comfort, and be our teacher and guide. Ministering spirits are angels of God who have supernatural strength to give protection from the enemy. We see that God has thought out what we, his children, will need to go all the way with this walk with Him. *"But as for me and my house we will serve the Lord" (Joshua 24:15). God bless you!*

Chapter Six

Slothful and unprofitable servants of God

The parable of the talents teaches that preparedness is not only an attitude of mind but also an investment of one's life in service to Christ with risks. Disciples are to work faithfully. When Jesus does return, there will be a triumph for the followers of Christ, for which we will be individually rewarded. As followers of Christ, we should take on the characteristics of Jesus. A new life in Christ is proof of the sincerity of our faith. Whom God bless is indeed happy. God does give his people blessing; the person who receives God's blessing is truly happy.

We need to hunger and thirst for the things of God. It should be the character of every believer, and Christ promised we would be satisfied. Our heart should be pure; that purity is not measured by people's practice but rather by God's character. When God measures a person to determine one's acceptability, He measures that one by His own unchangeable, unalterable, absolute holiness, and all who do not attain the standard of God's absolute holiness are unacceptable in His sight. One who has received righteousness from God is constituted as pure in heart and acceptable to Him, and Christ promised that those who possess purity that conforms to holiness will see God.

When Christ left to ascend to His Father, He left each and every one of us a responsibility to handle. When He returns, it is up to us to show that we have been productive in His ministry, not laying around being lazy and waiting for His return. When He suddenly appeared to find you hadn't done anything to help with the kingdom, and in return, you began to say you were waiting for His return because you know He is a hard God, and you were afraid, so you decided to wait on Him. And you really didn't know what to do because you had no one to instruct you on how to go out and minister to the needs of others. Because of laziness, the Father will tell you that you will not be counted as a faithful servant and will end up in the enemy's camp, facing the same penalty he has. You have no one to blame; God has sent his people over the earth to preach the gospel of His return. You heard but wouldn't listen because you were involved with the cares of the world and not the cares of God's children. You could think then, but when the day to stand before God arrives, you finally forget you suddenly have amnesia, your brain has stopped functioning, but Jesus says, "Too late, I will only be taking my children that is and will be faithful and believing." Don't cry and fall to your knees maybe kicking too! It's too late! We had plenty of time, and the decision was up to us. God does not force anything on His children; the decision is up to us. Who will you tell? It is too late; the only one left to tell is the one who will receive the same judgment you will be getting. Get ready and stay ready. "Who will you serve?" Forget about trying to play the game of amnesia on God; He is not the one He has your plan already cited.

Please use what God has given you, and you won't have to suffer the day or hour our savior will return. The day is near, and the time is here; be ready and stay that way. Laziness will not get you anything but death; you will share the sentence of Satan; although you said you don't like or wouldn't be his partner, you should have if we don't join in and share the work of sowing seed, bringing in the lost and the ones that may be undecided. The job is ours; the choice is ours, and the opportunity is available. There is a reward well worth the wait and the work.

Blessing of the Saint

Salvation is just for the ones who love the Father and all His provisions. Wait and see for yourself how wonderful that day will be when Jesus comes back for His church; get ready and stay ready. Don't forget we are responsible for all the gifts our Father has invested in us. Maybe you have one ability or many; however, use them, saint. Please take responsibility for the gifts God has given you. Multiply them, and your blessing will multiply, and run over that they will be much, you will have to go and borrow containers like the widow with pots of oil. "Elisha told her to go borrow vessels abroad from all her neighbors, even empty vessels. Do not borrow a few, but as many as she can" (2King 4:3). God will give you your deserved blessing because of your faithfulness; don't cut yourself short being lazy. Just remember that God didn't get up this or any other morning and decided He would not let the sun shine on us because He was lazy. 2 Thessalonians 3:10 says: "*For even when we were with you, this we commanded* you, *that if any would not work, neither should eat* "The Bible says that if you don't work, you should not eat, so let us do all there is to fulfill the will of God; we are responsible for each other. We are children of God, all colors and sizes; we are still covenant children of God. Don't let Jesus down. He hung on that cross for you and me and bled. Think about it, and He did it so that we may have life, and not only life, but have it more abundantly (John 10:10). Think about it and make your decision: are you for the work of the kingdom or are you going to be lazy about God's business? Your decision truly needs to be made right now.

Don't let the troubles of the world or the troubles of the flesh turn you around; seek everlasting blessings, not temporal ones. Pray always and seek that which is of God, and everything will be all right. The day is near, and the work is plenty. Let us not be like the slothful servant in Luke 19:22-26 and let Christ down, and He will turn His back on your future. It is important to make good use of God's gifts. When Christ returns, if you made no use of the gifts God gave you, He will say you are a wicked and lazy, unprofitable servant, and throw you out into the world with no protection, where there shall be weeping and gnashing of teeth. This shall all occur when we face the last judgment.

Imagine what He will say to those who use the gifts of God. He will say, "Well done, good and faithful servants, because you have been loyal in a few things, you shall be ruler over many." Please be like the faithful servants, where God says He will give all his inheritance. That is multiplying your gifts that will ensure your entrance into everlasting life with Jesus. We all are our brother's keepers, one for one and all for all; that's the Christian spirit that children of Christ should display when we are born again of Christ and not of the evil one. We are known by our outer appearance when we are born again with Christ-like spirit. Amen!

2 Corinthians 5:17 says, "If any man or woman be in Christ, they are a new person, the old is gone, and the new person is alive." We should not be concerned about our walk because we walk by faith and not by sight (Hebrews 11:1). Being visual sometimes will get us into a lot of trouble. Focus on Christ, and

all your strength will be activated. *"For us to live is Christ and to die is gain* (Philippians 1:21). One day, we who are alive and remain will be caught up together in the clouds to meet the Lord in the air and live with the Lord forever. (1 Thessalonians 4:17) We need to comfort one another as we wait because His return is a mystery to each and every one of us, even Jesus. Only the Father knows. So, let our walk be in the order with the teaching of God. Let's not hang our heads down with fear and shame when we come before our judgment day, being lazy about what God has appointed us to do. Let us hold our heads up and look Christ in the eyes with the expectancy of all the rewards we will receive. A laborer is worthy of his reward. If you are unsure what your gifts are, the Bible says, in James 1:5, "If any of us lack wisdom let him ask of God, that give generously to us without question ask, If we believe and doubt not. *"Every good and every perfect gift is from above, and cometh down from the Father of light* (James 1:17).

The most precious gift we receive from God is Jesus. If God shared His Son with us, would you think there is anything that He would hold back from His children? There is work in the field to be shared by each and every one of us, so don't be slothful; it is our responsibility to do our portion to see this through. The kingdom is ours for the reward.

Showing respect to everyone, loving your brothers and sisters, fearing God, and honoring Jesus. Continually multiply the gifts

God has entrusted you with because the Lord is not slow in keeping His promises. He is patient, not wanting us to perish, but for everyone to come to repentance and live forever with Him. Don't be slothful; that is not the thing to do. The job is ours, and we must see it through to the end. The reward is worth the wait. Workers are wanted, so come and see; you will be free. The Father is hiring each and every one of us to see this through. "O come and see" what the Lord has for you and me. He is so gracious and wonderful to prepare a new kingdom for you and me!

Chapter Seven

A forgiving God

Running away from God to the hog pen (world)

Ephesians 2:5-8: What we were once, but now we are saved through grace, not our own doing. Our heavenly Father is a forgiving God. From the beginning of creation, He forgave Adam and Eve for their trespasses when they disobeyed and listened to Satan. Through our first parent, sin entered into the earth; God's love for us made provision through His Son to give us a chance to receive the life that was once cursed. God forgave us through faith in His son Jesus. Adam brought death; Christ brought us eternal life. We have to be dead to sin and alive to Christ; Romans 4:7 says we are truly blessed. When we come before God with a clean conscience and ask for forgiveness, God will forgive us, cover our sins, and see them no more. If we continue to be imitators of God and live a life according to how Christ lived, we will continue to be able to come to the throne of grace because Jesus gave himself up for us as an offering and sacrifice to God.

God has a stipulation concerning sin. He will forgive every sin we commit except one, which is a sin against the Holy Spirit (Matthews 12:31, 32). We are like the prodigal son who asked his father for his inheritance and went to a faraway country; he wasted all he had living in sin. One day, he realized he had spent all his time partying. There arose a famine in the land, and he then realized what he had done. Sometimes, it takes things like this to wake us up; as long as we can do the things we want, we can't see, but as far as our money can go. He became hungry and decided to get a job. He didn't want one, but he was hungry and doing nothing. He found a job that wasn't the kind he wanted because he was accustomed to a better lifestyle but hungry. Stomach pain will sometimes make you do strange things. He went to work in a field, feeding swine that was detestable to him and his family, but yet again, he was hungry; he couldn't wait to get a paycheck, so he began to eat with the pigs. The Bible says, "If you don't work, you don't eat." There, he had time to think after his belly was full. He said to himself, "What in the world am I doing here eating food that nobody wants? When I was home, I ate better than this. My father had enough food for me and enough to spare.

If I continue to live here, I will die. He didn't have anything but himself, so he decided to go back home and began rehearsing what he would tell his father. How he had sinned against God and him and how he was not worthy to come back home and be his son again. I am going to tell him, "I will be your servant."

The compassion of a father

When his father saw him at a distance, he had compassion, ran, and fell on his neck. He hugged and kissed him with tears in his eyes. The son felt bad because of how the father had greeted him; he had disrespected his father's kindness, abused his life, and put a burden on his father. Regardless of his misconduct, the father greeted him with love and compassion as if he had never done anything wrong. Feeling low, weak, and ashamed, the son stood back and said with a loud, trembling voice, "Father, I have sinned against heaven and earth and against all your teaching. I am not worthy to be called your son. If I could have a position in your field house feeding your flock, I know I will be fed because I know I am not worthy." But the father was a forgiving father; he said to his servant, "Bring my son the best robe and wrap it around him, put the family ring on his finger as a sign I have forgiven him and that he has been restored, all his authority. Put shoes on his feet, which was a luxury only worn by the free man; the father was letting him know he was not a hired person, but a freeman. That night, to welcome his son back home, they had a celebration. The father said, "For this is my son; he was dead, and now he is alive again; he was lost, and now he is found." And they began to celebrate!

We, too, were once lost, but now we are saved through grace, not of our own doing, but through the blood of Jesus.

The Father sees us coming back to Him from a distance, and He runs to meet us happy with a smile on his face, welcoming us back. He begins to give us what we need to get our spiritual bodies back in focus with his. When we are separated from God, it is because there is something that is between us and God, and we can no longer hear or see the things of God. So we are separated from Him, but when poverty or whatever circumstances arrive, we can still see what God has meant to us. Sometimes, out of shame or unbelief, we feel that God has abandoned us, but in reality, we have left our first love. We feel like we can't come back and ask for forgiveness because of sins we have committed that are abominable unto God. We never think about how much God really feels about his children until the pains of life come upon us, and we begin our search for Him. God is a good, loving Father and expects us to live the same life as He lived, which is holy as He is holy. Coming back to God does not show weakness; it exemplifies strength.

The only way Satan can defeat you is to keep you separated from God, where you receive strength and power; we cannot fight the enemy on our own, and that is the reason why our heavenly Father has given us all the armor we need for the battle against the enemy. At all times, we have to be fully armored to be ready for Satan and his army, not by our might but by the might of the Lord. This is a spiritual battle; the enemy is here to steal your life and to kill or to destroy (John 10:10). Whatever it takes to separate you from God, who loves us and makes provision for us. There is nothing in our life that we don't receive under the blood of Jesus. It opens doors in our lives to bring us into reality, the things we need to survive. Sometimes, we might not receive as we think our heart desires, but we get what we need. So wait upon the Lord, and He will give you what you need in all areas of your life. Maybe we all are not financially rich, but have you ever thought of it? You have other things in your life that make up for riches that you cannot take with you. But seek the kingdom of God, and all these things will come unto you. Being rich is not for us all because it can be a destroyer if we don't know what to do with it. Like the prodigal son, he spent all his money on the things of the world and came back home out of shame, hungry, and broke.

Timely Blessing

Our heavenly Father knows what we need and will give it to us when we can handle it. If we focus on getting things from the Father, then we are not able to hear what we can do to help others who might have a need far more important than what we are asking for. If we stay focused on things we think will make us happy, we open doors to the enemy, especially if God doesn't answer prayer for these requests. If Satan gets you down, it is hard to receive strength to get up and fight; stay focused; this war is not about us; it's about the new heaven and earth that the Father will set up for the strong ones in Christ, so stay focus on your calling and not on your petition to God, which will keep you blinded, leaving an opening for the enemy to steal your joy and then your life. So, we shouldn't focus on ourselves but on God.

Stay out of the hog pen and stay in the grace of God, building up faith in God and not the riches of the world, which sometimes causes destruction to the mind and body. We sometimes don't know what to pray for, so pray the sinner prayer (Matthews 6:9-13), and there you will find all our provision from God, and the rest of our needs will come in order. Please do not fall into temptation. That is the reason why when Christ was on the Mount of Transfiguration, he told his disciples, "Can't you stay awake? Don't succumb to temptation; if you lose focus on your purpose, the enemy will come in like a flood, sweeping you away from your calling." We all have a calling. That is the reason why we need to find out what our purpose is here on earth. What responsibility the Father gave us, do the best you can with that, and you will receive a greater one. If we cannot be responsible for a small task, there's no need to trust us with more responsibility.

Don't become like the servant with the talent that went and buried it because of laziness and tried to put the blame on God, your reason for not multiplying his money. Sometimes, we need a scapegoat, so why not use God? Whatever happens in your life, God will always be your Father. He is a loving, forgiving Father. He began fatherhood from the foundation of the world and will not change now. He is the same today and tomorrow and will be the same forever. But don't test Him. You don't know what you are doing. He is a wonderful, loving Father, but to test Him is another story. So why not come back to God and don't stay in the hog pen. He is waiting for us with outstretched hands, waiting to take us unto His bosom and cover us with the blood of righteousness.

The parable of the prodigal son represents the repentance of a sinner being restored back into God's family through the ministry of Jesus. If we openly confess our sins to God with repentance and humility, He will remember His covenant agreement, and we can count on Him to forgive and forget.

Chapter Eight

Aspiration for Christ is expressed

Help me, Oh Lord, have mercy. It is me, Oh Lord, standing at the door waiting for your mercy. Help me to understand your ways, Oh Father. It is me; the days are here to be counted; let me count the ways. Lord, help me count the ways of your mercy and goodness.

Count me worthy to come unto you with open arms. Cast me not away from your open arms. Have mercy on me and spare me. Have mercy upon your child. Come and see what I can see, and take me home with thee. Take me now, and let me see how precious you are to thee. "Oh, how sweet is your name, take me home with thee. Calm me, Oh Lord, calm me. Tenderly are you calling; the earth is crying for your call. "Oh, take me home with thee. O takes me home with thee. There are times I want to see, but take me home with thee.

Swing low, sweet chariot, take me home with thee. "Oh Lord, won't you hear me calling you? Won't you answer my call? Please hear me today while I can be seen. Take me home with thee. Tenderly am I calling you, take me home with thee. "Oh, hear me now while I can be seen; take me home with thee.

Days are cold, and nights are warm; take me home with thee. Tender is thy mercy; take me home with thee. I am on the channel of; forget me not, take me home with thee. Swift is the feet of the one calling you; take me home with thee. Sweetly, I am calling you; take me home with thee. Birds are nesting in the tree; take me home with thee. "Oh, how high is your love; take me home with thee. What are your ways to reach thee; take me home with thee. Choose me, Oh Lord, choose me now. I want to hear your loving voice; take me home with thee. Have mercy on me while I am here; take me home with thee. There are others who need you to stand in the gap for us; please do not pass us by; stand in the gap for me. The time is here to obey your call. I am here, too! I am here to surrender to you; please don't pass me by. Standing in the gap for me, I am here to hear your call; please don't pass me by.

Dear Lord, please don't pass me by. I hear the birds are calling you sweetly and gently; please don't pass me by. I am watching you and gently standing; please don't pass me by. The days are warm; the nights are cold; please don't pass me by. Sweetly, are you calling; don't pass me by. Why, Oh Lord, are you calling me gently? I am answering you; I know your voice; I want to go; please don't pass me by. The day is here; please hear me, don't leave me, and don't pass me by. I am calling you gently; I am calling you; hear my tender voice. I am yours; can't you hear me calling you? My arms are open wide; I can see you; please don't pass me by. Grey is the cloudy days, and dark is the night; please do not pass me by. I want you; I need you; please don't pass me by. Tenderly, I am nearing you. Please don't pass me by. "Oh Lord, please do not pass me by. I am singing out your praises; please don't pass me by. "Oh Lord, please don't pass me by. Shall I come to you, or shall I wait? I don't know; please don't pass me by. I am calling you; please don't pass me by.

Trains are fast, buses are swift, please give me what you want me to take so I can come to you. With the expectation of seeing you now, please hear my call, and please don't pass me by.

There are horns blowing, and I can't understand the call. Will you please help me understand the call? Oh, Lord, help me understand the call.

There are different voices, but I want to know yours; please help me discern your voice so that you won't pass me by. High, high are the hills, low, low are the valleys; how sweet are the fields, why "Oh Lord, are you leaving me? Please take me home. I am calling you, please don't leave me, please take me home. Rush to one with the expectation of taking me; I am here for the asking. Oh, smile at me and show me your favor; I love to see your smile. Casting down, Oh casting down, shows me what you expect of me, and I will do it. There are many things I can do; please don't cast me away.

The wind is blowing gently. Oh, how I see your face. Oh, gently, I see your face; it is so wonderful that I can see your face; it is a face of love, peace, and joy. Oh, how I see your face. Running and prancing through the fields because I have the joy of the Lord! I have the joy of the Lord! I am trembling with joy because sweetly you are calling; sweetly and gently are you calling.

Chapter Nine

To Surrender To God

"On the wings of a prayer, Jesus talked to me, and now I am no longer the same. He talked to me, and He said that I am His. Walk with Him, and your life will no longer be the same. It is a choice you will have to make, one that will help you to achieve one of the greatest things in the world. Walk with Him and talk with Him, and you will see. Your life will become new. Tell Him what you want, and He will listen to you and lead you beside the streams of still water, where there will be peace of mind, and you will see. Walking and talking are not the same; try Him, and you will see. Just a little closer walk with thee. Go the mile with Him, and you will see how sweet it is to thee.

Walk with Him, talk with Him, and you will see. Go on to thee, and you will see. The Lord is calling you. Can't you hear his call? Listen closely, and you will hear him calling you home. Sweetly is He is calling you; listen to His sweet voice calling you. Come, Oh, come to Him, children. You might not know what to do, you might be confused, but let Jesus lead you the way. Let not your heart be troubled. If you believe in God, you will believe in Him also. He is the gentle one who is calling you. The day is here to hear his call;

come on into the call. Oh, look to Him, and you will see what you have missed. Give Him the chance to lead and guide you where you need to be. Oh, Oh, I need you. Swift is the feet of the enemy; he is calling you too, but only to destroy you; don't listen. There is nothing he is saying that is worth listening to. You will be destroyed if you do.

Jesus said, "I am the way to life; follow me, and you will see the light that will lead you to the place where you will find what you have been seeking." The walk of a righteous man availeth much, but of the wicked is not worth the count. There is destruction all around them. Be righteous as God is righteous; there is a reward of life and happiness to the fullest, and you won't be misled. Look to the hill where you will receive the strength that you want and deserve. Lord, I know you love each and every one of us. So please let us count the ways and see how we can enter. Sweetly and gently are the steps of a righteous man. Walk your way into the heart of God, and you will see what I am telling you. There is all you want and need. Oh, taste and see what the Lord means to you; don't take my word; try Him for yourselves. You will tell everyone about your walk with Jesus, how wonderful it will be, walk, walk, walk; even the same is something worth checking out to just see where it will lead you. I am sure you will never want to turn around and go back to the dry and unpleasant life that we all have experienced in our lives. Hear the birds; they are singing a melody to each of us, helping us see how sweetly He is calling us into the presence of God. He provides for them; they have no care in the world, and He will do the same for us, too.

Listen, let not your heart be burdened with the cares of the world; believe in Him, and you will see. Let us depend on Him for our every need; you will see how great he is. A mighty Father in times of problems and a loving Father when there are no needs. He will listen to you just ask and see. He will never turn His back on us if we harden not our heart like some has done in the past. Let's not follow those because there will be problems in our lives that we will have to contend with; I am sure with the world the way it is, you are not seeking any more to add to what you have. If we listen and be obedient, we will not have that mountain to climb, we will be able to go around. We make our life harder than it should be by making wrong decisions. Which, at the time, seemed like the best without asking God. If this is right, what should I do? We are no longer by ourselves or a burden to God. We are the sheep of His pasture. He cares for us. Praise goes to God! Amen.

Chapter Ten

Walking in the light

We are the children of light because we walk in the light; we are a city on a hill where our light may shine and be seen by men so that our Heavenly Father will receive praise (Matthews 5:14-16). If we walk in the light, we will receive salvation, and our sins will be cleansed forever.

Our Father is waiting and willing to take us in; our life is so important to Him. The time is here to be cleansed and washed with Jesus's blood. Come and see how good God is. He is waiting to carry us home. The time is here, and the hour is near. Be ready to enter; please come and see what He has for you and me. Watch and pray, for the time is here; salvation is at the door, waiting for us to knock and come in. Jesus is saying, "Oh, come to me, my children; I am waiting to love you and take care of your needs. Tenderly, I am calling to you: sweet is the chimes of a wind blower, and sweet is the voice of God. He is calling and calling; can't you hear his voice? So tenderly is He calling. Don't let Him pass you by. Today is the day to listen and be counted. "Oh, how wonderful His provision is for his children that have the heart and mind of God. Only they can inherit the kingdom of God ."1 Corinthians 6:9-10 says, *know ye not that unrighteous shall not inherit the kingdom of God? Be not deceived: neither fornicators, nor idolaters, nor adulterers, nor effeminate, nor abuser of themselves with mankind nor thieves, nor covetous, nor drunkard, nor revilers, nor extortioners, shall inherit the kingdom of God."* So don't be deceived by the voice of the wicked one. Salvation is at the tip of our tongue; please don't let Him pass you by. Swing low, swing chariot; He is coming to carry us home. Harden not your heart as at the time of provocation. When Jesus comes, be ready; our reward will be worth the wait. When He comes, we will know it; there will be destruction over the earth, but we will not be harmed. He will spare us because we are His, and He is ours.

Jesus is saying, "Come, my little sheep, come to your father; I am preparing a place for you where not anyone may come. The pasture is green, and the wind is cool; it will be yours forever, no more pains, no more crying." Revelation 21:4 says," *And God shall wipe away all tears from their eyes and there shall be no more death, neither sorrow nor crying, neither shall there be any more pains: for the former things are passed away.* He is coming, be ready, don't wait. Procrastinating is very dangerous. He has what we need; there will be no wants. The hour is here; don't take any chances with your life. Save it for what responsibilities God will share with us and all that partake of these provisions. Our heavenly Father has plans for His special children that take the walk of faith down to the plains of righteousness. No one can give what He has. "Oh, come and see what our Father has given us."

The day is near; peace has come, and we will enter in unto his grace. He is waiting. He has joy and peace for us just for asking; there is nothing that we will lack; come and see. The lambs are fed and don't have a care, so wouldn't He do the same for us? Trust in Him, and we will find the same security that He gives the lambs, flowers, birds, and all living creatures of the earth, for He cares for us. Swing low, sweet chariot; He is coming to carry us home. How many days are not what He wants us to look at. He wants us to beware of the enemy that will keep us from coming so that he may claim our lives. We are a big target; don't be deceived; he will use whatever he can to take us with him. Can't you hear him laughing with no compassion for you or himself? His time is near; destruction is close, without a doubt. "Beware, beware, I am warning you." He is seeking someone to devour; he will sift us like sand until there is nothing left to sift, and it will be too late because we will be on our own, with no one to pull us up, and then we will die. That is not what God intended for His children. He is sorry for what has happened, but it was taken out of His hands in the Garden of Eden through the disobedience of our first parent and put into the hands of the enemy. But God has a plan; He has the last word. Things are getting ready to turn on the trickster; his hour is arising, so be ready, stay prepared, and we will see the salvation of the Lord!

Walking in disobedient

Read the account in Exodus 14:1-31: Pharaoh didn't believe, but when the Red Sea opened and closed on his army, all he could do was hang his head down in anguish. Was he not warned? Did he not listen? Sometimes, we are so wrapped up in doing our own things we cannot see before our hands, especially if it will not benefit us. But when the final challenge arises, we will look kind of abused, but it's our fault. Lives will be destroyed, but God has given us his words. He also gave us different preachers to tell us what we have to do to get saved. The rest is up to us.

Please listen, don't be like pharaoh so you won't sit and hang your head down in disgust because your focus is on what you see now, not what is to come. Watch and pray as I tell you this: His words will never fail. Sodom and Gomorrah were given a chance; how hard did God's servant Abraham pray for these people, but to no avail. As he prayed, they became wicked; the only thing God could do was to destroy the city, to keep that kind of filth from spreading throughout the world; fire will cleanse and destroy. Lot's wife did not listen; God told them not to look back on their past and to look forward to what He will provide. His wife defied God and looked back; he destroyed her with salt to preserve her soul from being destroyed. God is preserving her for the final judgment. Read Genesis 19:1-29: Some of us won't listen. He will have to bring some kind of judgment against us but not destroy us. Sometimes, we fall away. He could destroy us, but He will give us another chance to make things right with Him. He is not hard to deal with because He could wipe this world clean. Satan is hoping that is what will happen because his day is near; without a chance, there will be nothing God will do to give him another chance. His chance is over, and there is no debate on what will become of him and his angels. On the final day, they will be thrown into the lake of fire to cleanse God's earth of filth, like He did in Sodom and Gomorrah, and His people won't have to be concerned by those pirates dirtying up our new heaven and earth. Fire will cleanse, and we won't have to be concerned about any of those diseases surfacing again. God is here, and Satan is here; who will you be choosing? Be careful about your decision. If your choice is wrong, you may have to live with that until you are zapped away with fire with no promise of return.

Prepare for the promises of God

Get ready for the time to be on the right side with God, the champion of the universe. Power is in His hand. Satan has no power; what he has, we, as Christians, give it to him out of ignorance. That is the reason God sends people out to spread His good news, so we won't have to be deceived about the tactics of our enemy. Don't listen to him; give him a closed ear, not an open one. It won't take long; if you start listening, you will be hooked on lies and become confused. Don't give him the time of day if he asks you anything; don't wait to see what he is asking. Tell him to get behind you and plead the blood of Jesus over your life. And I tell you there is no if or but about it; he will flee and fast. The blood of Jesus is the power He left us here on earth to use whenever we need it. Also, we have the protection of angels at your disposal. Use what God gave us to help us with our walk in life. Because with the curses that Satan and his demons left here, we will need it without a doubt. These provisions are here just for the asking.

We don't have any excuses to run away with the enemy unless we harden our hearts against the provisions of God. Don't do that, it is dangerous. Can you imagine what Pharaoh was thinking as he sat there in that chariot and all the things Moses had warned him passed before his eyes? Don't wait to see this; it may be too late. Grow up and do it on the winning team. Don't be a loser like Satan. It's easy to get in trouble, but it is hard to get out. There are always consequences; some are easier than others, but life itself is full of consequences. Try to avoid them if possible, and you will be able to live a productive Christian life with a wonderful future and a good hope of enjoying what God said he would give to those who serve and obey him. Amen!

The people God sent to us are not sent to waste our time; they are here to let us know what we have to do to be saved. So when that day comes, and we stand before the final judgment, we can't say we didn't know. The Father will look at us and say didn't I send you a person to explain to you what you needed to stay out of the camp of the enemy, and you, blinded by what he was saying, started walking with your head high into his camp. They are laughing, saying here comes another one of them they don't understand, don't know this is where you come when you are ready to burn with us. They won't turn their back to laugh at us; they will do it in our faces because if you are walking in the camp, you know without a doubt what they are laughing at because the jokes are on us. So don't be misled; don't wait to look up and see yourself entering the enemy's camp. The joke will be on you. Amen! Don't think you will be able to turn around when you march in; you will be enlisted in the army of destruction. Just like you enlist in our army, you just can't enlist and decide this is not what you want and turn and bounce out. You enlisted and will have to stay. It will be better to join a branch of service instead of the army of the devil. It's too late; he will kill you before you get out unless you have some help. If you are there, you have not prepared yourself for the battle, no armor or sword, just yourself;

enter in this way that is not going to help you. So, let us do what we need to help us stay out of the camp of the enemy. No visiting or even wondering what they are doing if we enter; prepare to die. His power is not like God; Satan is not a dummy, but one thing he does know is who our supreme being is, and when you mention His name, all the demons in hell shake and tremble, and you can hear their bones knocking.

The Bible says in Isaiah 54:17, "*No weapon formed against us shall prosper.*" If it was not so, God would not have said it; we can take that to the bank and deposit that and be sure it will draw interest. Amen! So be a covenant child of God, enjoy all that God has given us, and beware of the camp of the enemy. Don't go near it; beware of those wolves in sheep's clothing, too, and they will help you find it. Amen!

When you walk in the light, it blinds the enemy, and you don't have to be concerned about those wolves in sheep's clothing. They will flee because your conversation is always praised by God. Amen. That hurt their ears, and they want to stay as far from you as possible. So, saints of God, let us continue saying the things of God and not things of the devil. God bless you!

Chapter Eleven

Developing Faith in God

To follow Jesus, there is a cost! Jesus said, "Unless a man forsakes all, he cannot be my disciple." He gave an illustration about a certain man who prepared a feast and sent his servants to bring in the guests. But they all began to make excuses for not coming. One said I had brought some land and must go and see about it. The second said he had brought five yoke of oxen and was going to test them. The last said I have married and cannot come. When the man heard these excuses, he became angry. He told his servants to go into the city street and bring in the poor, the maimed, the lame, and the blind; also go into the highways and hedges and compel them to come (Matthews 22:1-14). He said none of the invited guests shall ever taste my food! Jesus said, "To be my disciple, a man must give up everything he has, even those he loves the best: his wife, his children, and all his family. He must even be prepared to give up life itself; anyone who does not carry his cross and follow me is not worthy to be my disciple." If He chooses you and you are unwilling to follow, He will replace you with someone else.

Followers of Christ will go through rocky situations; the road is not always smooth. God gives us authority over our lives through Christ Jesus. So then faith comes by hearing and hearing by the word of God (Romans 10:17). *And the apostles said unto the Lord, Increase our faith. And the Lord said, if ye had faith as a grain of mustard seed, ye might say unto this sycamine tree be, thou plucked up by the root, and be thou planted in the sea; and it should obey you* (Matthew 17:20). Believe in Jesus and His words will give you the power and strength, to do, as we will. Focus not on our strength but on the strength of God. When our faith has gone as far as it can, there is still power in His word; the Bible says seek, and you will find, knock, and the doors will open unto you (Matthew 7:7); it stands for faith, too. He is our rock and shield; we need not be afraid of asking. He is willing and able to give what is free to receive. When there comes a test upon our faith, let the Lord enter our hearts; He will fill us, and we will be able to run another day. Just keep asking and receiving, and we will one day win the prize He has for the one who wins the race. The race is not to the swift, nor the battle to the strong (Ecclesiastes 9:11), but it to those who endure to the end (Matthews 10:22). He is a rewarder of those who diligently serve him. Without faith, we would fall by the wayside and be destroyed. There is only one sure way, and that is Christ. Peace will never be ours here on earth, or good health we will never have. But Jesus said, "I go away to prepare a place for you, speaking to those who place their faith in Him, I believe, and trust

God. My Bible says the Father does not lie (Numbers 23:19). The things of the world will keep us in bondage, but faith in God will free us. Seeking the things of God will lead us to the place where we will lay around heaven all day. There is no reason for us to be lost or confused; the reason He sent His word to us is for us to seek and find the provision He has for his covenant children. Just knowing that being a follower of Christ brings life and being a follower of the trickster brings destruction should be enough to motivate us to have faith in God.

Living by faith

These are days when we need to have our faith strengthened; we need to know God. God has designed that the just shall live by faith (Romans 1:17). Any man can be changed by faith, no matter how he may be shackled. I know that God's word is sufficient. One word from Him can change a nation. His word is from everlasting to everlasting.

There is nothing impossible with God. All the impossibility is with us when we measure God by the limitation of our unbelief. Jesus says, *"What things so ever ye desire, when ye pray, believe that ye receive them, and ye shall have them" (Mark 11:24).* Desire toward God and we will have desires from God. He will meet us on the line of those desires when we reach out in simple faith. To activate our faith, we have to become a new person. When Nicodemus came to Jesus, he said, *"We know that thou art a teacher come from God: for no man can do these miracles that thou doest, except God be with him.*" Jesus said to him, *verily I say unto thee, except a man is born again, he cannot see the kingdom of God." That is born of the water and spirit, not the flesh* (John 3:1-10). If we are oppressed, we cry out to God; it is always good for people to cry out. You may have to cry out, and He will hear and answer your cry. God is compassionate and says, *"Seek the Lord while He may be found."* He has further stated, *"whosoever shall call on the name of the Lord shall be saved" (Romans 10:13).*

Every day, I would continue to follow Jesus and walk according to if I am to continue to be His disciple; it was hard. I knew that if I stumbled, He would be there to hold me up if I desired Him, too. Putting your faith in man, there is a possibility of being let down, but by putting your faith in Jesus, you will accomplish your faith goal. Every day, I was getting acquainted with the Father, learning to hear his voice, and putting my faith in God. "One day, I was walking, and the Spirit of the Lord gave me a quick warning that danger was near. I didn't know where it was coming from. My heart began racing, but I knew that Jesus was with me. All of a sudden, the Lord warned me about danger approaching. I looked up, and there was an enormous and ferocious rottweiler on the loose, which stood almost as tall as an adult. I was afraid even though God was with me, I made a decision to put my faith in God and trust Him. I looked at the dog and looked around to see where I could find refuge because God gives us senses to be used, not just to carry around like a garment. The beast was on the loose, galloping and growling like something in a nightmare, coming my way. I stood still, frozen; in an instant, I heard the voice of the Holy Spirit saying, *"Set your fear to the side,"* God's Spirit said to me, *Don't run; look the enemy in the eyes and tell him to stop in the name of Jesus."* Before I knew what was happening, my fear had turned to anger. I stomped my foot, and I told him, "Now, In the name of Jesus, get away from me." He stopped with a jolt as if the earth trembled, looked at me, and I looked at him with no fear; he then turned. I couldn't believe how strong the power of God was. That was one time faith stood its ground. By faith, believe that the power of God will protect you from any enemy tactics.

As I continued to face all the trials of life, I was able to build more faith in the blood of Jesus, what He says, He will do. We will never have to wonder if He will perform. When our faith is tested, God will be with us and bring us forth. We will be stronger in our belief that he will give us that mountain-moving faith that we will never have to question whether He will show up. The next time your faith is tested, without a doubt, you will not even stress about it; you can be sure because you know that faith has been built up in us and has placed us in God where we should be. The Father is very pleased; all the glory goes to Him, not us.

We have a wonderful God, a Father whose ways are past finding out and whose grace and power are limitless. I know nothing is impossible with God. He is a rewarder of them that diligently seek Him (Hebrews 11:6). For example, the man born blind: As Jesus and his disciples were passing by, they saw a beggar blind from birth, Jesus anointed his eyes with clay made with spittle and said: *"Wash in the pool of Siloam."* The man obeyed, and his sight was restored. It was not in the clay, it was not in the spit, but in the man's faith. That is what made him whole; that's powerful! If he had any doubt in his heart, he would have continued to lie blind and beg. Later, He found Jesus and could see and cried, *"Lord, I believe" (John 9:1-44).*

Faith is what is going to make each and every one of us whole. Make sure of whom you put your faith in. There is only one that you cannot duplicate, so make sure that man's name is Jesus. Who has all authority in heaven and earth that has been given to Him from the Father, so don't be deceived.

Chapter Twelve

Pure and holy before God

Before coming to God wholeheartedly, I was not pure. What I am speaking of is that I became like most people who look after the cares of the world, ugly and dirty inside. My life was not given unto God but to the adversary (Satan), focusing on the things that are not in the perfect will of God. I was like the woman at the well who had five husbands, but the one she has now was not her husband. (John 4:7-25) I had been in several relationships seeking love and not finding marriage. One day when I finally came to the end of my search, looking for something I couldn't grasp. I turned to the master, who had the master plan. He did not turn His back on me. He said, *"Come in, my daughter; I will give you rest." My yoke is easy, and my burden is light, come, come to me" (Matthew 11:30).* I knew his voice, and He was calling me home where I belong. I knew this was where I would find what I was searching for. All I wanted was to find love. Here it was just for the asking. My body and mind needed to be totally cleansed and purified with the blood of Jesus. Ephesians 5:5 says, *"For this ye know, that no whoremonger, nor unclean person, nor covetous man, who is an idolater, hath any inheritance in the kingdom of Christ and God."* Through my journey, I prayed and sought His face every day, no longer living as I had been before. I could not mix the things of God with the things of the world because I was convicted, even if I had a bad thought in my mind. Each habit I had, I began to un-robe, throwing away and cleaning out my physical and spiritual closet so I could come before God's presence and walk with Him. God will not walk hand in hand with the defiled of the earth; we will have to be pure and have the desires of God. He is holy, and we should be holy because 1Thessalonias 4:7 says, *"God hath not called us unto uncleanness, but unto holiness.* He is seeking man's righteousness, not the trash that man has accumulated. If we are to walk with God, we need to spring clean our physical and spiritual house. The pureness of our body is what we should desire and keep. Our lives will become an example to others who may pass us by seeing only God in our lives. That is what God wants of us: to set an example that He is not able to do because He is Spirit and not flesh. You will have to be a child of God to see the things of God. So, our job here on earth is to show Christ's likeness in us. To be pure and clean is not a hard task to perform; it is similar to our everyday living. The only difference is that it is clean and pure and will keep our body and mind clear so that the enemy cannot infiltrate. We will not have to get up every day wondering what will go bad in our lives because we will live under grace and not under fear (Ephesians

2:5). He is offering that to each of us to take advantage of. Pureness will also give us the strength to run this race for God, and will give us the opportunity to have a long life in Christ.

God has set every one of us aside for His special use when we are clean and pure, pure as snow, which is white, meaning a spiritual child of God. We don't see the pureness like we don't see God, but it exists because we see it in our daily walk with Him. He cannot set aside anyone who has fifty desires and does fifty things to their bodies. Man may not see these things that we do behind closed doors, but God does, and that should be enough to make us ashamed, especially if we seek after righteousness. We are only fooling ourselves, so let us clean up our act and do the right things. Christ is holy, so the church also should be presented as holy. Each and every one of us is a little god. In Genesis 1:26, God speaks about our image as His. If we are gods, we have a responsibility to ourselves and to our brothers and sisters and, most of all, to our Father, who graciously gave each and every one of us this opportunity to be gods in the universe. What an awesome God we serve; that is something we need to shout about.

Wash us whiter than snow

Each and every one of us who wishes to be holy should be washed and cleansed with the word of God. David said in Psalms

51:7, "*Purge me with hyssop, and I shall be clean. Wash me, and I shall be whiter than snow.* David knew for God to be with Him, he needed to be cleansed, and so do we if we are going to join the army of God. Pure as snow is what each individual will be when the blood of Jesus enters all of our bodies and flows from head to feet. Wash us, Lord, until there is no more to be clean. The way is to put on the boot of righteousness and gear up and follow the one who will bring victory to us. Faith in the blood is what we need and will receive just for the asking. There is power and victory; ask and believe, and you will receive (John 14:13-14). Nothing is impossible for those who believe in the "Most High God."

When I began to receive this revelation, my hardship and trials began to not hold me hostage as they had in the past; some trials still exist, but I am no longer bound. When they surface, I remember what God has said to me. I am a child of the most high, and He is responsible for meeting my needs. He didn't supply all of my needs but the ones I needed. I knew I was washed and clean with the blood and his word (Revelation 1:5). I had nothing to fear. I would remind the Father what He has promised me because I am His child. There were times before I became an adult in Christ, I would get so angry at God when a trial arose that I could not triumph, but the Father knew I did not know any better, so I think He would pray for me, too. He knew one day I would learn that He was for me and did not want any of His children to perish (2 Peter 3:9) but enter into what He has for us.

When we get angry with God for what Satan has set before us, that is the trap he enlisted for us to put distance between us and the Father. When we sit and think about it, we will see the set-up. The Father is a Father, like every one of us, a real parent. We do not go out and fight every one of our children's battles, but we teach them how to fight for themselves because we are not going to be with them all the time; they need to learn and take control. And that is the same way our Heavenly Father is to us. The trials of life make us strong; no one really wants them, but it is something we have to endure. One thing we must remember, as was said in past times, is that God would not forsake us. Pray for the pureness of our body and mind, and God will do the rest. It is a hard lesson, but it is one that each of us, as a child of God, needs to experience.

Just think about when we see snow falling on the ground, on the trees, and everywhere; that is what we look like inside when we are cleansed with the blood. That is the reason God is able to use us in the things of God; we are beautiful, without a doubt. "Glory be to God! What a terrific feeling to know that our inside is so beautiful. No defect, nothing so He can enter in. Nothing to hide! Nothing to be ashamed of! Then we can hold our hands up and say, "Come in, Lord, and sup with me, and He will." What a glorious feeling to experience having God live on the inside of us. He has made His home there because we desire Him. When we go to sleep at night, when we arise, He is still there. "Sweet Jesus! Every time we breathe, He breathes; He is there to help us each time we do. "I love Him and will continue to let Him live in my heart, soul, and body. That is the only way I can go through any trials of life that come my way, knowing He is here with me; my trials are His trials. What a wonderful thing to know; I am not in this thing by myself. I can see another day, each day that I arise, whatever the trial may be. I walk with Him, and I talk with Him because I am His own. I was bought with a price on Calvary; I am no longer my own, but God's. He has to carry my burden, especially when it becomes too heavy for me.

Let us follow the example of Naaman the leper (2 King 5:1-19), the king's army captain. He was asked to obey one of God's prophet, Elisha, against his will to bathe seven times in the river Jordan, and he would be cured. His servants persuaded him to obey Elisha, saying: If the prophet had ordered you to do some great thing, surely you would have done it?" So Naaman went down and bathed himself seven times in the river Jordan; when he came out again, his flesh was like that of a child, and he was cured of his leprosy. Let us also learn to obey and be cleansed with the blood of Jesus. Get clean and stay that way; it is the only way we will survive. "God bless you."

Chapter Thirteen

To become a living sacrifice

Romans 12:1 says, *"I beseech you therefore, brethren by the mercies of God, that ye present your bodies of a living sacrifice, holy, acceptable unto God, which is your reasonable service."* Overlooking the lake of fire, liars, thieves, and gamblers are waiting to enter. The lake is being prepared for those disobeying God's laws (Revelation 21:8). God's children will not face the lake because of their obedience to God. The lake is prepared for only the ones that are not prepared to follow God's laws. The lake is deep and wide, burning hot with brimstones and fire (Revelation 19:20). This is not the place you will want to fall in. There is no return.

People get ready; the day is near and close, and destruction is on the way. Keep your distance from the lake, stay on the side of righteousness, and you won't have to be concerned about the destiny of falling in. Grace is sufficient from God, and He is willing to keep us from the lake of fire. But we will have to follow the laws of God, keep our minds on the things of God, and practice what we preach. Think about the lake of fire; it is not the right decision to go that route. Stay with God, and without a doubt, you will not enter. Prayer and supplication are things to do to help us be strengthened and become bold in Christ.

The boldness of God is the first step to keeping us free from the things of the world. To keep those things on your mind is bad for you and bad for God because He does not intend for any of His children to be destroyed, but He would like for us all to enter into everlasting rest and peace with Him. It is the place He will prepare for each that obeys His laws. It is another thing for the disobedient one. Please beware: God is warning us every day in His words to keep us from stepping into the pool of fire. Listen and be prepared for the deceit of the devil. 1Peter 5:8 says, *"Be sober, be vigilant; because your adversary the devil, as a roaring lion, walketh about, and seeking whom he may devour:*

He is ready to prepare us for the destruction he will be receiving. To become caught up is a terrible thing to do. Listen and be patient; our day of delivery is near. We serve a very good Father. He is the shepherd of sheep and the caretaker of His pasture. He will keep us in whatever situation we may enter and will carry us through just for being obedient to the end and just for the asking (Matthews 7:7). Ask, and you will receive, knock, and the door will open unto you; don't tarry around. Read Matthews 25:1-13 the parable of the ten virgins. Don't be foolish like the five foolish virgins who didn't have what they needed when Christ returned; they had to leave and come back. They could not wait and pray, but entered into temptation and were forgotten.

Be prepared and stay that way. Don't worry about tomorrow or the next day of His coming; He will return. You just wait and see; our deliverance is closer than what you or I can see. A light is shining to show us the way so we won't have to be stumbling around in darkness. God always makes provision for us so that everything we have to do is made easy for us to accomplish what we have to do. So don't be foolish and be left behind. Join the winning team, have a smile on your face, and enter into God's grace, being proud of your accomplishment. God is not asking us to do the impossible. He has prepared us for our deliverance and has given us the tools we need to use to help us on the way. It is not difficult to be obedient; it is what we all should want to do; giving our body as a living sacrifice, holy and acceptable to God, should be the responsible thing to do. A pure, clean body is what God expects from each and every one of us.

In 1 Corinthians 3:16, Paul said, *"Know ye not that ye are the temple of God, and that the Spirit of God dwelleth in you?* Clean up your body; it is the temple of God; sweep it out with the blood of Jesus, and make sure the blood of Jesus continues to stay flowing within the temple of God. And we will not have to keep on cleaning up. God cannot live in an unclean temple because He is a God of order. When we are not clean, He keeps his distance because He just can't use us the way He would like. Ephesians 5:27 says, *"that he might present it to himself a glorious church, not having spot, or wrinkle, or any such things; but that it should be holy and without blemish."* Spotless and without wrinkles is the way we should try to present our bodies to God and continue to be a living sacrifice.

When there is a call on our lives, God is willing and able to use us in the area; if we are not clean, He will pass us by and choose another person to perform the will of God. 1 Kings 5:3: David wanted to build His temple, but God rejected him because he was unclean; he had hands of bloodshed, so God passed him by and chose his son Solomon. That is the same way with us; if our body and mind are not clean, He will pass us by and use someone else who is equipped and whose house has been swept clean with the blood of Jesus. Don't let Him pass you by, saints of God. Sweep out your temple with the blood of Jesus and keep it flowing, and you won't ever have to be concerned about anything that is not like Jesus entering.

Our body does not belong to us; it belongs to God. We are using it as a loaner, so let us take care of what belongs to God, and there will be no reason for us to destroy what God has graciously let us occupy until He returns to pick us up and take us where we belong. The filth of the world will destroy us, and it will also hurt the Father, for each and every one of us who perish. John 3:16 says, *"For God so love the world, that he gave his only begotten Son, that whosever believeth in him should not perish, but have everlasting life."* He does not want any of us to perish (die) but for us to come to repentance and stay that way. "Grace, Grace, Grace! Oh, how I thank God for His wonderful grace." Without it, saints of God, where would we be, and how would we know the way? Grace is the way, the blood of Jesus is the way, The Father is the way, and the Holy Spirit is the way. Catch onto either one, and you will ride home free; the transportation will be easy and smooth to ride, with no bumps or knocks to shift you and make you fall, no reason to fall off. Just hold on for the long haul, and things will be okay if that is what you want. The choice is yours and mine; make the right decision, and everlasting life is there for the asking. Freely given if you ask for it, the price is a fair one; it is free, and it's not free. Nothing comes without a price. This one asks for a clean house God wants and deserves. We are His sheep, and He is our shepherd. He will lead us into victory, just wait and see. They say sheep are dumb, but they know their shepherd and will follow him because they know he will take care of them and give them the food they need. In Psalm 23:1, David says, *"The Lord is my shepherd; I shall not want."* We are like sheep; we should follow the example of David and follow our shepherd, and he will give us what we need and deserve. We no longer need to just survive. In John 10:11, 12, Jesus said, *"I am the good shepherd; the good shepherd giveth his life for the sheep. (27) "My sheep hear my voice, and I know them and they follow me."* When sheep are taken care of, their coats are nice and white so that the shepherd can use them; I don't think he can use the coat of a damaged sheep. So with God, if we are damaged and unclean, he cannot use us; He will pass us by. 1 Thessalonians 4:7 says, *"For God hath not called us unto uncleanness, but unto holiness."* So, saints of God, keep your body clean and acceptable to God, which is our reasonable duty to God and ourselves.

There is a reward that no one else can give to us. Here is a chance to receive life and receive it abundantly (John 10:10). That is the joy of the Lord! Stay clean, stay ready, and stay alert of anyone trying to enter and dirty your house. If we keep our bodies clean, anything that is not like Christ won't and cannot enter because the blood of Jesus will be flowing inside the things of God. The enemy will not cross; he can't, and he won't. A clean house and a clean temple are what God wants, and so should we. A cleansing every day is what God requires. (Leviticus 11:44) *"For I am the Lord your God; ye shall therefore sanctify yourselves, and ye shall be holy; for I am holy: neither shall ye defile yourselves with any manner of creeping things that creepeth upon the earth."*

Chapter Fourteen

Living a Christian life through trials

Living a life in Christ is not going to be without trials. The longer you keep your eyes on Christ, the more trials will come your way. If we pray and cry out to God every day, our walk with Him becomes more controllable. Don't wait until the trials of life have taken over and you can't think of what to do and are afraid to call on God because you are ashamed you have turned your back on Him. Keep the doors to Him open, and you won't have to be ashamed. He is our provider and the Father of the world to those who desire. Life is going to be rocky; there is no hiding place; the only refuge we can take is in the bosom of God. There is no other place where we, as covenant children, will find rest. Jesus is our rest; He is all we have and need. Trials are not to break us down but to give us the backbone we need.

God doesn't want any wimpy children; He wants ones that can fight the battle, whatever battle exists. The Bible speaks of only the strong survive. We have to carry some of our burden; when it becomes too heavy, we know where to find strength. We are like men and women who are training for a marathon. There are exercises you have to perform to build up those muscles; if you don't, you will not be able to compete. It is the same with the marathon of God; there are exercises that we, as Christians, have to perform to obtain the strength we need to run. Put on those spiritual shoes and all your gear and line up to start the program and exercise every day, not when the trials of life come upon you, but every day. Then, one day, when the spiritual marathon begins, we will be able to line up and be counted. Yes, we are in a race, a race to the end, where we will receive our prize if we run and win. So keep it up and place your heart and mind on the things of God and not the things of the world. When problems arise, and they will, remember to pray without ceasing. And remember that one day, all your exercises will pay off.

The more we pray, the more we will become the target for the enemy, and when it happens you can count it all joy because you know that your exercising is paying off. Your muscles will become stronger and stronger. When the arrow of the enemy strikes, it won't hurt you nearly as it has before; some will just bounce off because of the spiritual muscle.

There will be days when you will stand and wait for the attack to test your muscles to see if you are going to be able to stand. And at a distance, you will start running toward the enemy, so you will get the first punch and knock him down before he sneaks up behind you and give you a sucker punch. That is the way he operates. So beware of the enemy's tactics and stay strong in the Lord and the power of His might. *"Wherefore take unto you the whole amour of God that ye may be able to withstand in the evil day, and having done all to stand. Stand therefore, having your loin girt about with truth and having on the breastplate of righteousness." (Ephesians 6:10-18)* This is the armor of God. After your body has been toned, you can wear this armor God has given us. Puny warriors will not be able to hold this armor up; it will be too heavy to handle. This war is for the strong, not for the weak.

Can you imagine how Daniel felt when he was thrown to the lions? Because he would not worship any other god but God Almighty! Daniel had been exercising his spiritual body and was ready for God's armor. As Daniel kneeled in the den with the lions, God sent an angel and shut the lion's mouth so he was not harmed. They knew he served a mighty God who protects his people from any trial the enemy brings upon them when they obey him. The king's men saw Daniel the next day alive and well after spending the night with the enemy. They knew he served an "AWESOME" God who does as He says. He is alive and not dead! He lived within each and every one of His children. So let us live our lives as Daniel and pray and believe so when the enemy attacks, we won't have to kick and run because of the trials of life but head toward those trials so that God will fix them and prepare us for the next one to come.

The battle is not ours

We as children must realize that Satan really doesn't want us; he wants God, but he is not strong enough to tackle him, so he goes to the next thing that is close to God, and that is his children. If you ever want to go to war with a father or mother, you go after their children, and you will see the strength that has never surfaced; it will become a big war with no end. So if we just remember the war is not ours but God's (2 Chronicles 20:15), we are only bate to Satan. Life is what God gave us to live to the fullest, so we can't run around concerned about what is going to happen, but we can live life according to God's laws. His words will keep us together so we will not fall apart and possibly end up in a sanitarium or on medication. What God said He would do, we can depend on it, and He will not fail us if we do our part. I am not saying things are going to be exactly as we want all the time; there will be days that will be wonderful and days we will wonder if we will make it through. That's when the spiritual body goes into action. Then you pick up the armor and gird yourself and hold your head high and remember who you are and who your father is, and that will give you the strength to pick yourself up and look the enemy in the eyes and tell him, "No Satan! Not today, I have my armor on, and I am willing to carry it, so you do what you have to do, and I will do what God wants me to," and turn and go the other way, leaving whatever trials of life that have tried to sucker punch you. He will turn and go after someone else who may have left his or her spiritual armor. He will return, and you will be waiting with more power than you had before. I think each time we win a battle with the enemy, God rewards us here on earth with more power because each time we defeat the enemy's tactics, the next time he comes, it will be with more force. Therefore, we will have to have more power to deal with what he brings. So keep your armor shiny and intact to defeat any trials that may come our way, and you will be ready to receive the prize God has for you. Amen!

To destroy one's body, which does not belong to us

It is not over after death; you destroyed only the house you live in. The real person still lives on with problems more severe than before that you will have to deal with. Life itself continues in the spirit realm; the penalty is not at its end. To take one's life is abominable to God and yourself. Your life was not yours; how can you steal that precious, most holy thing from God? The wages of sin is death (Romans 6:23), eternal death, and no resurrection to eternal life. You don't really understand; you think it is all over, but the final day when you will be judged is when you will pay the price. What is called death is the everlasting punishment that God will serve you, and there will be nobody to be destroyed; it will be your spirit that will be tormented. It will be better for you to suffer here for a little while than to have everlasting suffering with Satan and his demons. That is going to be the second and last death for man, and you will not want to go through that. You might not believe it, but you will receive it. Jesus shed His blood for each and every one of us; what purpose did you find in that? Did you know, believe, or did you not want to receive? It was not done only for a show. Why did you crucify Him again? When you take your life, the blood is sacred; it does not belong to us; it was bought with a price on Calvary (1 Corinthians 6:20).

What was so important for you to leave this world to go where you cannot hold up because where you are going will be tougher than where you left off? It was a waste of your time. The problem is you let Satan come in and rob God. Keep God on your mind and not yourself, and you will be able to survive and not have that abominable thought on your mind. How do I know? I was once riding in the same boat you are. I came from a dysfunctional family seeking love and acceptance in all the wrong places and found none. I thought one day I had found what I had dreamed of, someone to love, someone to cherish; it turned out to be a mirage. My life was like a carousel going round and round with no complete stops. I was searching for something, feeling lost and blind, betrayed by all that I thought I loved. I was looking for answers in the wrong places, getting no responses. Later, I began to conduct myself in the manner of my peers, with drugs and alcohol, whatever! This is not the life for me, and I wanted something better; I didn't know how to find it. I was completely confused.

There were times I thought the way out would be to end it all. I began to pray and didn't know if God really existed. This was the time for me to reach out and to find out. I had not been a Christian, and I didn't know if He would hear a sinner's prayer. I didn't know how to pray or to reach God. I began to do my best, and He heard my cry and saved me. My life will never be the same. Having faith in God is hard, but if we work on it each day, it will become stronger. That is what they say: that only the strong survive. Satan had me exactly where he wanted me, lost in my own ignorance. If I had only known who God really was, I could have broken the shackles off my life much sooner.

Satan is a thief, and each time one of God's children lets Him come in and rob Him of us, that puts a smile on the enemy's face and puts a sad expression on God. All we have to do is to keep an open communication with God, pray, and stop thinking that God doesn't exist because He does. Look around you. How did all the worldly creation appear not by itself? You are under the attack of Satan every day; he will work on the minds of the weak ones first to win their thoughts and to take their proudest possession, which is their life. God is so proud of each and every one of us. That means the breath we breathe is the breath of God.

There is no age limit for Satan to pick on; he looks around to seek the weak and keeps punching them until he has them under his power, and then he will be able to snatch your life from you because you listen. That is why God said if anything comes to your mind that is not of God, don't listen.

Whose voice do you hear?

Recognize the voice of the enemy? Avoid any conversation with him. How to avoid that is to learn to hear his voice and start praying. Ask the Lord to give you a dumb ear to the enemy's voice, and He will. To know who is talking to you is to know what kind of God we serve. Listen to the conversation; if it is about your problems or about anything that is going to make you unhappy, then it is time to tune him out. Don't wait until he finishes; stop him in his tracks. Tell him to get away from you and plead the blood of Jesus. If you are unsure of what he is going to say, don't wait around to hear the lies he is going to feed you; tell him to get away, and he will flee. You might not be a church person or someone who is in the right standing with God; He will honor you just for the attempt of trying to find Him. Give Him a chance, and you will see; if you give other relationships, friendships, and any other ships a chance, then it's time to give God the same opportunity.

A wonderful, loving God will never ask you to do anything as drastic as blowing yourself up or taking something that will separate you from the life He has freely given you. When the enemy comes to you, he doesn't let you know the full deal about your life because he is a con artist out to accomplish one thing in life: to steal, kill, and destroy (John 10:10), and when you take your life, he has accomplished what he wanted to do. Don't get caught up in the enemy's schemes. He does not have our interest at heart; think about it: there is only one who really cares for us; it is our Heavenly Father. There are trials that develop in our lives, and we are not able to conquer them; that is why our Father has sent us all the provisions we need to beat the problems.

I see people that have not lived their lives to the fullest; they stop and give up. I asked myself what kind of problems they could have that caused them to give up and destroy what did not belong to them. If it is the pressure of our peers or parents or maybe friends, put them out of your mind; we don't owe anyone anything but God, the giver of life. What Satan will do is send people close to us and give a message of destruction as if you are failing in life. When the ones you know are doing this, get some space from them. Don't listen; it is not of them, but the enemy is using them. That is the reason, at times, you hear the term "love them at a distance," because you don't want to stop loving them because they may not know that the enemy is using them, saying things to you that are going to push the button of destruction. They only think you need to hear this to reach your goal in life. But in true reality, they are being used by Satan to destroy you.

So get away from them and maintain your distance. One day, when you are stronger, you will be able to rebuke what they are telling you. When you destroy your body and not the spirit, which really is your life, you put a lot of people in mourning. That is a good way for Satan to blame God and tag around like a thief and a robber and try to sneak in and do the same as he has done to you, getting more people under his spell while they are vulnerable through their grieving. It's a set-up. Can't you see the pattern? Don't let him get away with that; we can stop him right now.

Education Is Life

If we, as God's children, let everyone know about the evil one, we can bond against him. That is why he is working so hard to keep God out of the institutions where children are because I was told what children learn from birth to five years of age, they will use that knowledge to build their lives. When I was a child, if you did not learn or hear about God at home, you most definitely heard about Him at school or other places that provided care for children. The younger generations of today are not able to learn about God in many places other than church and home because Satan has used people on every level to make the name of God like poisons that will kill and not bless us in every area of our lives.

Everywhere you look, there are controversies about where God can be and where He does not belong. We are in a war, and it's not our battle, but the battle is of the Lord! (1 Chronicles 20:15). We are soldiers who have to fight the battle of God for our freedom and also for the lives of our children; they are our future. We are somewhat back to the Pharaoh era when he sent out a decree against the Jews to slay all newborn males, saving all females at birth. Moses's mom saw that he was a godly child, so she hid him for three months; when she could no longer hide him, she took a basket and laid her infant in it and put him in the river to save him from the slaughter of Satan, not knowing if she would ever see him again (Exodus 2:1-10). We are still experiencing the slaughter of children now, but in a different way; the slaughter is the same.

Oh! How dreadful things are for our younger generations, who are supposed to be our future? What can we do, or where can we turn to receive the justice we seek? There is one answer to that question, Jesus! Jesus! Pray always for our nation and our president. Pray for the unanimous office of praying congressmen who will rule and make laws for our country based on Biblical principles. That will be the only way we will be able to catch hold of our country and bring God back into the lives and hearts of our children. Let us stop letting our children make Pokémon, Superman, or any of these characters become their gods and teach them who their Heavenly Father is, which is the true and living God, and that there is no other true God. Let our children know if the one that they may believe is god can't live forever, then he is not God; our God cannot die!

If we say that God is supreme over us, our lives and souls belong to Him, we don't have any right to it. We will stop the bad, terrible behavior of our children living such violent lives. They have no respect for authority, their lives, or anyone else. We are in a dilemma, a lost situation now. All Christians will have to pray together in unity to save the nation from the enemy.

The strength of the world is lost, without a doubt. If we can show them that this is not all there is to life, maybe we can save them. If you look at the world it's not a pretty picture to look at. Their minds don't have the capability to look further than what they can see in front of their face. We, as Christians or followers of Christ, know the road map; we have been shown the life-after-death provision. We know and understand that God has something better for all His children after this war is over. We will have to persevere until the end of this system, *and God shall wipe away all tears from their eyes; and there shall be no more death, neither sorrow, nor crying, neither shall there be any more pains: for the former things are passed away (Revelation 21:4).* Our children want this too! Without a reason for doubt, how will they learn if they do not have a teacher? Don't wait until it's too late. Teach them after birth while they are unable to speak the way we can understand. You won't get completely through to them, but I believe if we can tell them that we love them and they understand and give us a response with a smile. If we tell them that there is a man named Jesus and He will always love them and say it often, I believe it will become real to them. Don't wait until school age, and they pick up the garbage they hear and be taught; teach them the vital things that will help them filter through their brain to determine what is of God and what is not. Our children are smarter than we give them credit. The Bible speaks about our generation becoming weaker and wiser. If we look around the world today, it is visible without a doubt. So I leave with you what Solomon, the man of God, has to say in *''Proverbs 22:6; "Train up a child in the way he should go: and when he is old, he will not depart from it.*

Chapter Fifteen

A Soldier of the Lord set aside for God's special use

When you enlist in the army of the Lord, you will have a responsibility to God and yourself. Your obligation will become a daily task; people who once were your friends will become your associates. And Satan will stage more attacks because you have clothed your body with the uniform of the Lord you have enlisted.

One, two, three, get ready; we are joining the army of the Lord; buckle up; this is going to be a long haul. Prepare for war without ceasing. No one knows when this will end, only God. Be prepared; the hour has come; hooray for victory. We have joined the winning team of God. I can hear the trumpet horn blowing, and the enemy will be defeated. Get your Bible and get your gear; there is a time to be prepared and stay that way. There will be no turning back because if you do, the door of service may be closed on you. Don't look back; just keep on marching, keep on the beat with the march of victory. Be prepared and stay that way. The word of God is what will keep you fit, so be prepared and stay that way; it will help keep you in the service of the Lord without dropping out.

Get your armor; get it fast, and keep it shining and clean to protect yourself from the darts of the enemy. He is throwing them in all directions; you will not be able to watch because he is full of tricks. So you have to stay suited up for this war if you are intended to last. God will prepare you; you have to listen if you are going into the battle of the Lord. The battle, at times, is really hot, but if you are prepared, you will last until the end, run into victory, and win the prize God has for each and every one of us. I can see the enemy marching; I can see God's army marching; the attack is on the rise. Be ready; you have joined the winning team. Don't worry, you will survive. Keep in step, and you will see that victory is ours. Join the army of the Lord today, and you will not be defeated. God has a special gear for his people that not anyone can wear; we are special people with special gear. The enemy is in sight; we will not run away but run toward him, not allowing him to get away. The righteous will never be defeated, so don't be in despair; the war is ours; it is the war of the righteous, not the war of the evil one. They hear you marching; they are afraid because they know you are a child of God. *"Put on the whole Armor of God, that ye may be able to stand against the wiles of the devil (Ephesians 6:11-18)* because our time of victory is here. The battle is here for us at the hand of the righteous. There is no one to challenge us if we look the enemies in the eye and trample on them. Don't give them any leeway because we are the righteous who have been given the authority over them if we don't give our authority away. We are winners and not losers. We are in the army of the Lord. Hold your head up, press on, and know every victory is for the winning team. Our captain is a winner who has triumphed in every war He has been in. So be prepared to march into victory.

In Joshua, in the sixth chapter, when the army marched around Jericho, they knew the plan; they knew the victory was theirs. They did not fret; they did not cry. They marched in and took the spoils of the city without any bloodshed, and so will we. Victory over the enemy, "O, how sweet that sounds. Can't you hear the triumphant walk of the spiritual boots? Marching into the enemy camp to come out into victory, Get ready and let's go; the battle is already won!

Chapter Sixteen

Learning how to pray

There is a solution when there is a doubt about what we should pray for or how we should pray. One day, the Lord softly said to me that when in doubt, the model prayer is sufficient. The first thing we need to do is recognize whom we are praying to. *Let us pray, "Our Father which art in Heaven, Hallowed be thy name. Thy kingdom come Thy will be done in earth, as it is in heaven. Give us this day our daily bread. And forgive us our debts, as we forgive our debtors. And lead us not into temptation, but deliver us from evil: For thine is the Kingdom, and the power, and the glory, forever. Amen (Matthews 6:9-13).* This is the simplest prayer for anyone to say, and our Father will respond to this prayer quicker than anything you can pray. Your will and His will will manifest. Praying to the Father is something each and every one of us has a responsibility to do. It will keep the door of communication open to the Father. Pray without ceasing (1 Thessalonians 5:17). Is this the correct thing to do? Our prayer is the door to open to the Father and the key to our success to reach Him. Through prayer, the needs of everyone may be sought. The Father is a merciful God. He does not intend for anyone to learn any special formula for a prayer. The model is sufficient than any prayer we may send to Him.

The authority and the power of this prayer are supernatural for everyone. It was taught to Jesus' disciples (Matthews 6:5-18), and it still has the same power that it had then. Praying this any time, day or night, is the key. The more we pray, the more doors will open to us. When we were children, we prayed a model prayer for the little ones. Today, we as adults can also pray this. God is so special He will even accept it: *"Now I lay me down to sleep, I pray the Lord my soul to keep, if I shall die before I wake, I pray the Lord my soul to take. Amen.* Without a doubt, whoever wants to pray this to the Father will also open revenue unto the Father. Praise God! He is always opening doors for His children who humble themselves before Him and come as they are, even as small children; there is no age limit to Our Father. He is a Father forever; we are His babies who should always need Him. He is not partial to prayer; God does not sit and hold a whip over us and say this is not acceptable because there is no age limit to prayer. Praying is the thing each of us has a responsibility to God and ourselves. If we have set aside a personal prayer, He will also hear that. How we communicate to the Father is up to us. The two prayers above will open just as large and wider doors as the special one that every one of us has prepared to present to the Almighty God, who hears us all on whatever level we may come. There is really no position but to get the full effect and get God's attention quicker. If we are on our knees, God gets all the honor and glory, and we will also receive it. There may be circumstances in which our knees are not responding, but God will honor that, too. He will not turn a deaf ear to your prayer because of position. He is a wonderful shepherd, and we are His sheep.

Praying to the Father is a release of what has occurred in our daily walk when we know not what to pray for. We can pray the model prayer, and all our needs fall under this prayer, as well as those of others. It is a complete petition in itself. It was not in the Old Testament because God's Son was not in the Old Testament. He appeared in the New Testament with a new will for God's children, having better provisions that help keep us from living in bondage trying to live under the covenant of God. All prayers and everything else falls within a new, after Christ. Let's focus on God's Son, and you can't go wrong. He is the life, and the life is in the blood. Everything He did was for us; there is no reason for us to try and figure that out. Praying to the Father is communion with Him without a doubt. Every one of us should find time every day or when time permits. Praying to the Father, the Heaven will open, and God's blessing will shine down on the earth and touch every one of us. Praying for our neighbors, we will become intercessors for the people of God, reaching all His children and providing for their needs. Praying out loud is a great practice so the enemy will hear and stay at bay; it will hurt his ears.

Why do we pray?

There is supernatural power in any prayer you send unto heaven; you just can't imagine what goes on in the realm of heaven and earth as you pray. It starts shaking up things, and that is what keeps the earth standing as it has. It's the prayer of the Saints that availed much (James 5:16). Pray and be counted for being a child of God if you want to be counted also in the service of God. Praying is the key that opens doors to ministries that may not function as well as they should. It opens jails for those who may be innocent of the crime. It lifts people out of confinement, such as wheelchairs and sick beds. We might not know these things are occurring, but they are. That is the reason we pray, because of the power that lies in prayer.

We don't just commit to the prayer, but we release blessings to the nation. We are to keep our conversion of the flesh and reject things that are not like Christ. There is a fantastic revival when we pray; we don't know how many of us will be praying at the same time to God, causing miracles to happen all around us. If we hear of something that has occurred on the earth, just think about it when you prayed; some of that surfaced from your intercessory prayer. That's a miracle on its own. We need to pray and make this a better world for every one of us. The miracles are from prayer to the Father. When that happens, He responds and sends the angels into action with His Spirit, which is a force on earth that man cannot duplicate, and there is no reason they should. Prayer is powerful; don't be concerned about what you are doing; just pray and keep this a better place for us to live. That is a sure-known thing for us to do. Pray without ceasing means exactly as it says. Pray all the time to stay connected to God and your fellow men.

Intercessory prayer is not supposed to be a standard obligation of a meeting place; it is wonderful to do, but intercessory prayer is a shock wave when we, as individuals, pray. Wherever you may be and get things moving, it is just as powerful and even more, the merrier. There is no age limit on being an intercessor; the model prayer for the youth can do the same. It will reach out to those who are standing in need of help. There is no standard age limit for intercession. Teach the young to pray; they are also responsible for making great miracles happen on the earth. Their voices will be heard, and the action of prayer will jump into motion and make just as loud of a bang as the elderly person. Teach them now, and they will make great miracles when they become mature in the Lord. When they become an adult, they will be able to reach out more, stronger than before. Because practice makes perfect, teach them, and their days will become longer on the earth.

The wisdom of God will continuously be in their heart, and when they become older, it will not depart from them. They can shake this world up, too. There is no age limit on shaking things up for God. Pray that your voice can be counted as God's children; no one will be overlooked. It is a dynamic experience for every one of us. Every one of us is taught to vote; now, I am stressing to heart that we should also pray to keep our nation free from the tactics of the enemy. God and Jesus are in heaven; we have been given this job to perform here on earth; this is where we live. Take care of it. It's our responsibility, just like our homes; we take care of it and then do the same for the earth.

Praying Will Break the Yoke of Bondage

Praying is a wonderful experience; it does a lot for us as individuals.

To let God have all our cares at night or whenever we pray gives us a release in faith, so we do not have to wake up each day with so many things to add to the new day. Give your worries to God and start a fresh new day the next morning. I believe that our hospital and sanatorium are so full because we don't pray and truly give our cares of the day to God when we pray.

Release yourself; there is nothing we can do about the problems; give them to the Master and let Him handle them. When you start a new day, you can deal with what that day has brought and go through the next day with a brighter outlook. Don't add your problems from yesterday to tomorrow; that will become more than you can handle. The word said He will not put on us more than we can bear, but we are putting on ourselves more than we can bear.

He is the bearer for us to get a release from these problems. Are we truly giving them to God and releasing them to Him and not taking them back as soon as we stop praying, picking them up, and adding them to the new ones? After a while, we began to have a collection, and after that, I can see a breakdown. Give the problems of each day to God and let Him handle them. He is well able to provide. I know it is hard to do, but when you start doing it, things will become easier when you give them to God and know there is nothing you can do about it.

At first, it is hard to accomplish because old habits are hard to break, but day by day, set your mind on your goal. When you give them to God, and you know there is nothing you can do about it, you will make it when those situations occur, and they will. Replace the thought of Satan with the thoughts of God. Keep your mind on scriptures and verses; anything that will build you up and not down will make you strong. Thank God for what you have, and you will start planting seeds. After a while, you will begin to see something start to grow out of it. Worrying is the only way Satan can attack our minds because we are not able to think. It will become "What about me" and not "What about God?" Let us not center on "what about us," there are people that have more to be depressed about than us. We have our lives, and we have God; that is hard for us to see at that time, but in reality, what can you do about your problem but pray? Worrying has never answered anything!

Miracle through Prayer

I see every day now what I was told; I have worried about everything, and one day, I got tired. I began to look around me and saw that it was not all about me. And don't look at what your neighbor has because you don't know how long it took them to understand their problems and give them to God. Some people learn faster than others. We are all like babies going from birth to adulthood; we learn at different stages, but when we learn, God can hear our prayers and act on our behalf.

Then we begin to see the formula of trusting in God and casting our burden on God because He cares for us (1 Peter 5:7). Remember, take one day at a time; we are not going to pray one day and believe. We, as babies, are not going to get up one day after birth and begin to walk. There are stages in everything, so go slow and learn, or if you are a fast learner, do your best, and God will be there patiently to help you with your walk of faith. Pray for yourself and the nation; we can't get every prayer through. The Saints were praying for Peter, and guess what? He was in jail between two jailers, and the chains released him. The bars were open, and Peter was freed (Acts 12:4-17).

Prayer can do all things but fail. Prayer of the saints: There is power in the unity of prayer, praying from generation to generation, which is the reason the world is able to stand. Prayer is a door to open unto the mysteries of God, that a few will find the key, and it is sitting before their eyes; you have to focus on the purpose that God has given you. It is not hidden; there is no special formula that we have to figure out, but it is all in our prayer that the key to everything we have been looking for; there is nothing else in this world that will fulfil any of our needs.

Jesus is a model for prayer. Yes, He is the Son of God, but He is an example for us; when He prayed, things happened; when He prayed for Lazarus, he rolled out of the tomb, wrapped in his burial rags, bound by death, and Christ release him (John 11:38-44). When the widow woman's son died, Christ just laid His hands on him, and he became a living soul. (Luke 7:11-15). Adam, in the beginning, was without life, and the creator breathed the breath of life into him (Genesis 2:7). We don't realize what we, as prayer warriors, are doing with the backup of the most high. We are not able to perform anything without God. He is a miracle worker. Jesus prayed to the Father as He hung and died; it was not a prayer of vengeance but of peace. He prayed to His last minutes, keeping communication open to the Father, not losing that connection (Matthew 27:45-47). That is what we should do to follow the one who gave us His life, "Our Jesus!"

Chapter Seventeen

What is our duty toward our neighbor?

Matthew 7:12 says, *"Therefore all things whatsoever ye would that men should do to you, do ye even so to them: for this is the law and the prophets."* What is our duty toward our neighbor? The Old and New Testaments teach, *"Thou shalt love thy neighbor as thyself" (Leviticus 19:18; Matthew 19:19).*

If we want to know who our neighbor is, Jesus said in Luke 10:27 to love God with all your heart and soul, strength and mind, and your neighbor as yourself; this is the greatest commandment. Jesus gave an illustration about a man traveling from Jerusalem to Jericho, who was a Jew and was attacked by thieves, stripped of his clothes, wounded by them, and left half dead. A Jewish Priest came that way. When he saw the wounded man lying in the road, he looked at him in need and passed by on the other side, and soon after, a Jewish minister passed the same way. He went up and looked at the wounded man, saw he was alive and in need, and also passed him by. But a certain Samaritan, knowing that Jews hated the Samaritans, came to where he lay and had compassion on him. He bound up his wounds, bathing them with oil and wine, set him on his beast, brought him to an Inn, and cared for him. When he left, he told the landlord: take care of this man, and I will pay whatever you spend on him when I return. So, who is your neighbor? He who showed mercy; that is your neighbor. We are to go and do the same. The parable is intended to chasten self-righteousness. The priest and the minister have a responsibility to God and man to love their fellow men and to bring the word to man and man to God.

Jesus himself was the kindest man who ever lived. All the deeds of kindness that He did in three short years in John 21:25 says, *"And there are also many other things which Jesus did, the which, if they should be written every one, I suppose that even the world itself could not contain the books that should be written. Amen.* Jesus talked a great deal about kindness, just the plain, old-fashioned everyday habit of common kindness. Judging by what He said, He would rather see that in His followers than any other character trait. Not that our kindness will save us, but if we are ever saved, He saved us. Jesus put so much stress on this thing of kindness that He identifies Himself with those who need it, and in effect, tells us that we cannot be friends with Him and at the same time be indifferent to the suffering (Matthew 25:40-45). Jesus came to build a world of beings like Him, and when completed, no one else will be there. Jesus also said, *"And whosoever shall give drink unto one of these little ones a cup of cold water only in the name of a disciple, verily I say unto you, he shall in no wise lose his reward" Matthew 10:42).* Jesus said that not one single act of kindness, no matter how small it maybe will not ever be un-rewarded.

"Jesus said "this is my commandment, that you love one another as I have loved you" (John 15:12). Love is the power that rises from our soul's need. It drives us to seek another for our sake. It moves us to help another for his or her sake. Love seeks, and love gives. God's love becomes our love when he becomes the center of our life. When God, who is love, lives within our soul, His love reveals it in our everyday living. He becomes our power of love to see when there is a need for our brother or sister to respond.

The Power of Love

One day, as I became more wrapped up in the things of God and not myself, I was driving off the highway and saw a man with a tattered sign. I didn't stop to read what it said; the Spirit of God began to tug at my heart, saying there is your brother in need. I turned around and came back; the man was an unknown person holding a sign that read, "I need money to go home." After reading it, I passed him by again. Not finding peace within my soul, I made the circle again; this time, I stopped to see what the Lord wanted of me. I stopped my car, afraid, but not completely because the Holy Spirit was with me. I asked him where his home was, and he replied he was stranded and someone had attacked him at the shelter. I almost lost control. I held back the tears. I told him to stay here until I returned. I needed to get a ticket for Georgia, which was his destination. I forgot to ask him what part of Georgia. After I spoke to the attendant at the bus terminal, we exchanged information about how he had just bought a ticket for a stranded lady with children. That helped me understand this was my Christian responsibility. He asked if I trusted the man. I told him his spirit agreed with my spirit. I just want to get him home safe so we figure out the town that he lived in. The attendant ensured he would go where he said and could not cash in the ticket. That day, I cried going downtown and back, calling my daughters Connie and Peaches and speaking to them about this incident; they warned me to be careful, which was in my prayers. I returned with the ticket; he had the biggest smile and thanked me. I said to him, "God bless you." God's plans were perfect; he had time to catch the city bus downtown and to catch his bus home. The bus schedule was perfect; everything worked out according to God's timing. I knew God did it all. I received so much joy, as if I had won the lottery. I have looked for him but never saw him again; there have been others who stood in the same place, but God has not compelled me to stop. Who is my neighbor? All mankind is our neighbor that has a need. I thank God for giving me spiritual ears to hear His voice. I could have passed him by like the man wounded by the side of the road. That day, God chose me to be the Samaritan, and I obeyed. Whenever a situation may occur, and God speaks to us in that small, sweet voice, we should listen. There is a possibility this could be the day for us to be a Samaritan. Our street corners are full of our fellow men; if God does not tug at your heart to stop, just pray for them.

Who is our neighbor? A person that is in need is our neighbor. To have the Spirit of God in us, we will be willing to lend a hand to where there is a need. Jesus helped many people, and we, as Christians, should do the same. What if Jesus had certain people that he would help? Where would many of us be? He did not pick and choose. He only did what His Father sent Him here for, so likewise, we should do the same. He was one of the greatest people when it came to all mankind. He even gave His life for His neighbor, which was the noblest thing to do for His neighbor. We are no longer neighbors; we are children because of the blood that connected us to Him forever. Oh, how sweet that was for the grace of God and the grace of the Son. He could have changed His mind, but He didn't because of the compassion He had for every one of us. For Christ to live in us, we should have the same compassion for each other. How can you say you love Jesus whom you have not seen, and not love our brothers and sisters that we see here on earth (1 John 4:20)? Think about it: do we love Jesus? Well, if we do likewise, our lives should reflect His compassion. It should be seen in everything we do or say. Compassion is the love we enforce when we help someone. Just don't talk about love, but put it into action. Be a doer of the word and not one that speaks. Let your light shine before men, and let the love of Christ be recognized through us as being a testimony for Jesus.

The Bible says you can know His sheep by their deed. Let's not make Jesus a liar; let His word be true and not void through the acts of men. When you show love, you are a true disciple of Christ. The reward is given out of love and not show. Love finds its expression in service to fellow men (Galatians 5:13) and is the chief test of Christian disciples (John 13:35). All human love, whether toward God or toward man, has its source in God, it is created in believers by the Holy Spirit (Romans 5:5). As a sure test of our faith, we must love our enemy's as well as our brother and sister (Matthew 5:43-48).

Please don't be like the Priest and the Minister who gave an oath to God to serve His people. When an opportunity arose to serve, they turned and went the other way. Our love should be without hypocrisy (Romans 12:9). What then is our duty toward our neighbor?

Chapter Eighteen

Evangelism

We are all Evangelists, but only some have the gift of walking into the office. Every one of us has a responsibility to God and man to reach out and help each other. Tell them what God has put on your heart and how He has saved you. Pass around the goodness of God. That is all an evangelist is: people who work for the Lord, helping God save others who do not know about God's goodness. There is no special gift for each of us to do this job, only having the willingness to save souls. Through the love of God, we should enjoy helping others come to salvation.

The Father's Spirit is all we need; after we get it, we are to have the Lord's joy, which will make us want to share it. It is a wonderful experience to look back into one's life and see how many people we have told about the God we serve. Each time that is done, we are planting seeds and waiting for a harvest. Yes, we are all gardeners with the supernatural ability from God waiting to surface. Paul said, "I have planted, Apollo's watered;

but God gave the increase (1 Corinthians 3:6-7)." We are the same.

That is why we today have as many Christians as we do: because of the planting of the seed of God. And as every one of us passes by, someone else comes through and waters that seed a little more, and after a while, God starts letting the nutrient of His word penetrate that person's heart, and one day, everything that they have heard comes to pass. "Ok, here is a new man in God." Developing into a beautiful blossom, getting ready to go and tell everyone what they know about how God saved them and how they were lost, and God thought enough as He passed by and saved them. That's good news."

This is the Christian cycle of life; there is no pulpit with them, only the grace and love of God that is being shared because God and ourselves do not want any one of us to perish but come to the same fountain of life and drink and become whole and find life. Each day this process is done, you see that it is what keeps our brother and sister safe in the bosom of God. Get ready, people; we all have a simple job to do without any stress on our body or mind; think about it: we should be able to lie down every night and think about how many souls we were able to capture for the Lord. There is a great reward for everyone that we help save. That is a wonderful job; the pay is not always seen, but there is a reward that no one else can completely satisfy our soul. The Spirit of God will help you tug at everyone you bring into the sheepfold of God. All the work is not for one; it will be shared whenever a child of God comes our way. As we tell others about how we came to Jesus, there is a similar song and dance that we have performed to prepare to find the man who gives peace. So, let's share what God has given us.

The responsibility lies willingly with every one of us. There should not be a single day that passes that we should not share with someone about how God has saved us, if not a verbal word, but just how we greet people passing. That will make others wonder about your disposition, and the next person passes by with another characteristic of God. That very person passing could be suffering and lost. Seeking something they cannot touch, but in reality, it is God. Enough of God's people come by planting seeds; there are other lost souls for God; it is a glorious cycle of life. Keep on planting. It might seem that you have not reached these people, but each time you share with them the goodness of God, if you could see in their hearts, you would see this very tiny seed that has been planted. Praise God!

And you know what? One day, the seed might be one of the well-known Evangelists of our time and era or one after. See, that's what it is all about. Just look at the Billy Grahams of our day. A seed was planted, and someone else continually watered, and "Bang!! There, look at what we have done for the kingdom of God. We might not all become a big Billy Graham, but we can be Billy Graham Junior. That is just as good.

Get in the program wherever you can squeeze in and be counted among the ones who save. It is not all about being seen; we all cannot be chief, but a warrior is what God is looking for to go into battle and bring out the spoil. Put on your armor, get ready to go out on the battlefield, bring in the spoil of the land, and get it burned and pure for the God who saves thee. Evangelist is the name for all who go forth with the good news of God; you are sent into the Kingdom of God with a special purpose to save and to gain entrance into what God has for His faithful few. The twelve disciples of God were evangelists. God told them they are to become fishers of man, lay down your nets, and follow me (Matthew 4:18-19). What you will start catching will give you much better food than what you are catching because man does not live by bread alone but by every word that proceeds from the mouth of God (Luke 4:4). Go and save souls.

Harvest of Souls

Food is for the stomach, but souls are for God. Food is a temporary fill, but the food we receive from God will fill us till we want no more. And will stay, and we will never want any more.

That kind of food will save us from the wicked system we live in. We cannot be lifted from the vicious cycle in which we are living, but we can separate ourselves from the wicked ones of this world and still survive, knowing who we are and where we come from. Let's keep up the good job of Evangelism and lay our heads on our pillows, and if you want to stick your chest out and say well done, good and faithful servant to yourselves, I don't think God will be upset with you. As you rejoice, the entire heavenly host will be rejoicing with you. Amen!

That is the reason the Father wants us to study to show ourselves approved (2 Timothy 2:15) for the work that each of us has to do. We are not going out to share some garbage with our sisters and brothers; we want to share the truth of God with them. I am not speaking of you holding the people hostage on the street with your podium, preaching to them, but a simple scripture to let them know, "I go to church and enjoy it." I have learned in 1 Chronicles 28:20, that Jesus never fails. If they ask you where that is located in God's words, you will know. If not, lead them as close as you can. But we all know without a doubt that we once were lost and how He came and picked us up at the bottom of the well where it was dark and damp, with no comfort and pulled you out and cleaned us up, gave us warm clothes and a dry place to lay our back and freed our minds from the destructive things that throw us in the bottom of the well. That is a testimony that will raise the hair on their head. So please be a witness for God; it is not a very hard job.

When in doubt, and you don't know what to say, just whisper to the Holy Spirit and say, "Holy Spirit, what should I say to this person?" He will start talking to you. And you will see the light in their eyes, and you can be sure that is a sure catch. Evangelize everywhere you go with a casual conversation about God; do not club them in the head with your Bible and chase them down the street, trying to find a church and throw them in. Putting on the too-holy hat will surely push them away from the truth; they will probably say, "I don't want anything to do with that kind of a Christian group; something is wrong there. I don't want to have anything to do with them." But a kind and gentle step into their life is what will leave an impression for a long time. One day, that very person could be sitting in the pews next to you. Or maybe in the pulpit, there is no guarantee that we, as saints of God, could end up with our harvest because we plant and water, but God gives the increase! Amen!

That is what this is all about: caring and sharing with each other, not all about ourselves all the time. Don't get me wrong, God wants us to take care of our home first; if you are broken down, starving spiritually and mentally, you won't be any good for God. We need to be decent and have things in order to catch fishes for the Lord. Can you imagine going to a new convert and looking like you just crawled from under a rock or something, and you are standing there testifying about how long you have been in church and smelling terrible and saying, "Oh, how I love Jesus, I once was lost, and He found me and turned my life around. They will look at you and try to run the other way because they will say that if that is the kind of Jesus they found, I don't want Him. He is not a very good shepherd if His sheep looks like this. I am speaking about being on your best. You may have just got off work in dirty work clothes, but there is a charisma about a dirty working saint; that is a great difference from one who has crawled from beneath a rock; got the picture!

Being an evangelist, you don't have to prepare for the new convert; just stay ready and be prepared; you will never know when your opportunity will come upon you. Smile at everyone you see; that is a great start, even on days that may be more challenging than the others. A smile at someone else can break the chain holding you hostage. Evangelism has no age limit, which is a good reason to teach our children starting from birth. Let them go out and tell their peers of their surroundings about God, and let them be a witness. Many of their associates will be watching them, and they will be able to become younger converts through what they say and do around them. You had to start somewhere, so why not start while you are young? Some will be able to avoid some of the destructive things our youth become involved in. The youth will listen to them quicker than the adults because they are on the same level, and they won't say they are old and trying to make them old. Some of them will listen, some won't, but if we are equipped for all ages, we won't miss anyone. There will be a revival around the earth for us all; no one will be missing, and no one will be lost. We will all go to heaven and be with Jesus at the final call of God. That will be a glorious time, and we will be a part of Him; that is what will make this a glorious thing to know we are a part of something that will give life and not destruction. So, everyone should join in with God and make this a glorious place to live so that we can find peace in God. Amen!

Conversion of the Flesh

Conversion of the flesh is a process we all must go through. The body we live in has to be washed and cleansed with the word and the blood of Jesus so that it can operate on the same level as Jesus. Our bodies are not the same as God would want them to be because of the sin that was birthed into the earth, which contaminated all things, especially the things of God. So we are in a cycle of washing and making pure. Conversion of the body will take years of putting our body and mind through something called "the cleansing process." That is only the training of the mind on what it can do and what not to do. As saints of God, we cannot behave as we once had before.

Conversion of the body can free us and send us on the right path to freedom from the things of the world. God is a Father of order, so we must follow an order to become children of God and become pleasing to God. Conversion is like taking a bath in the blood, washing away the old man, and becoming a new man. It will not be blood in itself but a spiritual way of thinking.

Followers of Jesus will be bound to an oath to do certain things, like honoring our parents, God, and friends. If you make a pledge to God, you will converge and become new. This is a spiritual process; nothing will show up or be seen on the outside except the new person you will become, a Christ-like person walking in the order of God. Your footsteps will be ordered by the Lord (Psalms 37:23), and you will be like Jacob when he became Israel but no more Jacob (Genesis 35:10). Because we became a follower of God, we become someone else in Christ. This is the conversion that each of us must receive to be able to follow Christ. Our way of thinking changes with this baptism of the word and, therefore, surfaces a new you. Ready and to be commissioned to accomplish the job God has called us to accomplish in His name. It's not about us anymore but about God and His purpose. We receive the willingness to jump in and build, do what is necessary to please God by not holding back ourselves, and submit completely to make God happy with our submissiveness.

We all have to converse; we all have to be changed for what we are called to do. Paul speaks about putting on the new man when we become a new creation of God (2Corinthians 5:17). When an Ethiopian eunuch was baptized, he became a conversion of the Lord; something happened when he went into the water; afterward, Philip left supernaturally and showed up some place else, with the willingness to serve (Acts 8:26-40). We will show up. I don't know where, and I don't know when, but we will show up for duty.

Conversion is a quickening of our mind; it does not react as before, and there are things that surface that we never knew were on our brain. There is a sort of brain revival of things that somehow has been stored and suddenly released when the time comes for it to be released, only for the things of God. Not for anything we want to use it for.

We were brought with a price; we are no longer ourselves (1 Corinthians 6:20). We accept full responsibility for what God has called us to do. Conversion is a long word for convert; it's not different, only the process of cleansing with the process of cleansing with the things of God. That way, we are able to accomplish what we have been called for without any hassle. There is nothing to make us wonder what is going on; God will make it happen. There is nothing you or I will be doing except to become submissive to the will of God, and He will finish the job. Submissiveness is a long haul, but you can do it and will love what becomes of you.

There are jobs in obedience; obedience will not bring you into the spirit realm of being free of problems; they will come with the package, but God will give us a new way of fixing them when they arise. You will be able to go around and not try to go through putting them in the rear and not in the front. Conversion is a revival of the body and mind; it is an experience God shares with anyone willing to change and be a servant of God. It will not be forced on anyone. True submissiveness conversion will lift your spirit and give you joy in the middle of a storm in your life. Where there is a storm, you can expect a rainbow to follow, bringing the peace you have been looking for.

What was said, "the flesh is weak, but the spirit is willing" (Matthew 26:41). We have to keep our flesh under control because if we let it take over, we will lose our life to the flesh, which like anything that is not like God has the penalty of death. So the wages of sin is death (Romans 6:23). Death entered the earth through one man's sin, and through one man's blood, life entered too (Romans 5:12-21). What a wonderful process; the conversion of the world occurred before our naked eyes. Without that, we as saints of God would not have a chance; there is a conversion for almost everything in a different process; ours was through the blood, not of anything but of Jesus.

In the blood of Jesus, there are so many provisions for each and every one of God's children that know their shepherd; a sheep knows his shepherd, and so do we. We need to be washed! Washed, and washed every day in the blood and stay clean so that we will walk in the conversion of our body. You cannot do it with sinful thoughts or actions of the body; they will not mix. Your sisters and brothers might not know the thoughts of a man, but God sure does (Psalms 94:11). You will not be able to hide from Him. When Peter was on the rooftop, that was a conversion. God was opening up new revelations unto him, giving Peter a broader portion of service to perform (Acts 10:9-48).

You have to prepare your mind and get on the same level with God, and He will show up and use you supernaturally because you will be useable material and will become a miracle within itself. People will look at you, remember how you were, and say, "Look what the Lord has done in their life; "yes, that is what it is all about." The conversion will show up, and people will see it and want the same thing. Paul had a conversion experience on Damascus Road when he was Saul, and after his experience, he became Paul (Acts 9:1-31). What a conversion and God will do us the same way. It's all about the kingdom of God; we cannot get around it. Whatever God has to do to save us, if it is right, He will perform. We all have conversion experience; we might not understand it at the time it happens; some are mild, and some are little stronger, depending on the person.

I think God has everyone in mind, seeing if we can handle this or whatever, and what conversion is right for each person. In Acts 2:1, when Peter and the Eleven Disciples were in the upper Room, they experienced a level of conversion; they were waiting on the Holy Spirit to receive what they needed to evangelize the nation and bring in the sheep. Without that conversion, they would probably still be waiting for the comforter to come. When He came, they quickly began to disperse, went out, and started working in Jesus' name.

Conversion is the key to all of our ministry if we are to be able to perform the things of God in a proper fashion that will be pleasing to God. Wait for your conversion; pray for it, and it will show up; just watch and see. Listen for that small voice speaking to your heart. You might not understand, but what God asks of you, please perform, and you will arise a new person with duties that no one else can perform. We, as individuals, have different abilities that God only enhances with His supernatural power to give us the ability that no one else has.

We are individuals with different personalities and different responsibilities for God. That is one reason we should not try to see something someone else is doing and try to imitate it; that might get us in trouble. Do what God has given you, and there will be no problem. Why try to become a twin of a person who was born alone? If God wanted them to be duplicated, He would have done it at their birth. Be converse and stay a single person and begin to follow the leading of the Holy Spirit with whole submissiveness. Let go and let God take control; let Him be the pilot of your plane, and you will go places with the man who has the master plan.

The gift is free. God has one for each and every one of us who freely want to receive. Each and every one of us can get this by asking and praying. He will hear your prayer, and I guarantee He will show up and have the answer to whatever you need and want. I guess that is the reason it was said to try Jesus, the man with the master plan, for your life and mine. We don't have to be on the rooftop to receive, we don't have to be in the water, we can be where we choose and ask, and we will receive. He will change our way of thinking and how we live our lives, so let's join up with Jesus and have that conversion experience, walk into the light, and stay that way forever. Also, become one accord with the Father, the Son, and the Holy Spirit.

Chapter Nineteen

In Our Darkest Hour, How Can We Find Peace?

First, we need to start praying to the Father, asking Him to come in and give Us the strength we need to conquer this problem. We know that without His strength, we are not able to do this alone. Don't rely on your strength; please, this is a big mistake. The Father of all heaven and earth is there to take you through any situation; you have to pray and ask. The strength will come supernaturally, and you will wonder what happened to the situation that you thought was so big and there would be no surviving. There is nothing impossible for God; we need to depend on Him for everything and stop depending on our strength, which is the strength of a normal person. We are not able to carry out some of the problems that may arise in our lives.

The battle of the mind is a terrible thing to experience when you travel through different situations. It is so devastating when we are not able to bounce back and start where we left off. That is another hard impact on the mind. Sometimes, our mind can handle the blow; sometimes, it becomes weak, and we begin to fall. Our will is so weakened that without strength, we become bound with despair and misery and can't go on. Praying will be our strength; praying will be what we need to travel that highway of misery; it is a challenge in life that we, as individuals, don't need to try and do it along.

Please get stability from God; He will be more willing to come in and help. It doesn't make you weak to get the help you need from God; that's what He is here for: to give strength and comfort in times of need. It is the same with us as parents; we are here to give strength to our children when we can. Don't, please don't go alone on a journey by yourself when there is help for the asking. When you begin to sink from being burdened with problems you decided to handle on your own, sometimes it will be too late to pull out of the situation and ask for help. So before this occurs, get the help you need when you first enter the situation. If you get help earlier, you will be strong enough to stand against anything that comes your way. Don't wait until you are overcome with problems before you decide to reach out for help. It is the same way with a medical problem; when you first discover a symptom you may have, you will seek medical attention and make an appointment; if you are using good judgment, then you ask for help. The Doctor analyzes the problem, gets to the core, and prepares you for healing. That is the same way with God: go to Him with the problem, let Him take it, and dissolve it. You will not need to come to Him with the problem; instead, take the problem back and try to solve it yourself. When I say give, that is exactly what I mean: give and turn your back on it. When the final decision is made, you will be clear of it, and it should be forgotten.

God Is a Problem Solver

As children of God, we will not be immune to problems, and sometimes those difficulties will look like High Mountain and deep valleys. Don't try to climb them without being skilled in mountain climbing abilities. When the problem is deep in the valley, don't go in and try to find the solution; you might get lost. God is a mountain climber, He is a valley keeper, He has the equipment to clean it up, and no longer does the situation exist.

Dark is the problem; God has the light to shine in and make it show itself, and when it does, it will disappear. Problems like to hide and work in darkness to make you crumble, but when it has light, it becomes ashamed and runs away. That is why we need light in every area of our lives to make whatever is not like Jesus run away. We want the problem to dissolve and not part of us to waste away. Problems with different degrees can make you weak and stumble because of the darkness it carries with it. Remember, when you enter a dark room, you don't stumble around trying to find what you entered the room to locate, but you reach for the switch to turn the light on and find what you want. You are shining light on the problem, and when you do that, what you were looking for is located, and the problem is solved. Okay, look, that's the same with other problems; don't play around with it. Get the things solved, throw it in the recycle bin, and turn it into a blessing instead of a curse.

That again is a delicate situation about staying under the mantle of God so that we will be able to come to God in our hour of need without being ashamed of shunning God when we think we don't need Him. That makes it hard for us as individuals to go to God when we are in need. If we practice it daily, we will be more eager to reach out to Him in whatever situation that may stick its ugly head out into our lives. And by doing that, we can laugh at it instead of it laughing at us.

When David sinned with Bathsheba, he knew he had done what no man should have done to his fellow man. He might not have wanted to go to our Heavenly Father out of shame, but he did, and God forgave him. Throughout all of David's days, he worshiped God, put the sin he committed against Uriah out of his mind, and started a brand new day with God; 2 Samuel chapters 11 and 12. That was a critical situation he did not try to fix and waited around shame, but he went boldly to God and asked for forgiveness, and guess what? God forgave him. He will do the same for us, too. The Bible says you should ask, and you will receive; that means what you want is according to His word. That is one of the provisions of God; He can't deny us what He has promised us, His covenant children. We have a right because of the blood of Jesus.

Some of our sins can put us in the valley, and we need to know the way out; it will be through prayer. Don't let the valley become your God; you know who your Father is, then go to Him. Peace is what each of us needs, and we can't live our lives without peace. The joy of the Lord brings the music to our hearts that makes us want to run on and be the best we have to be. Peace is contentment; peace is what we need to be a weapon in our lives to shine on the problems that try to capture us. Peace is not going to let anything that is not like God hang around. Peace is a weapon that will destroy; peace is whatever is good and loving, and peace is peace. That is what God wants us to have in our lives.

Without it, where would we be? It is a scary situation to think that it would disappear; what would we hold on to? God is of peace (2 Corinthians 13:11), and if we are to be in His bosom, we will have to love and want peace to stay with Him. Peace is a part of our life that makes our spirit glow the lights that keep darkness out. Keep the peace, and you will be free of darkness. Darkness is a problem, and peace is God. As Joshua said in *Joshua 24:15, choose ye today whom ye will follow.* Peace, my peace, this part is of me.

Peace or darkness? I pray every day for the things of God, and that is peace. I don't need any darkness; it will only make me sad and put me in bondage. I don't want it, and I will not accept it. I am human; it will try and surface; my job then is to reach out and touch the master's hands in prayer and keep praying until I feel a release, not praying and looking for an instant answer but praying without ceasing. The problem is not what we want; sometimes, we need them to put some hair on our chest, a way of speaking! The more we struggle with it, the more we will break down, but the more we put it in God's hands, the more we get strength and find favor in God. He will be able to use us more in His ministry. Praise God!

How can We, As God's Children, Do All Things?

Philippians 4:13 *says, "I can do all things through Christ, which strengthens me."*

The strength of the Lord is the strength of power in our lives; we become spiritual giants. Our inner being becomes energized to perform whatever there is for us to accomplish. The strength of the Lord is a wonderful provision that God has granted His children. We can receive this strength; it is a supernatural ability. Our strength is natural strength; we are limited to handling some of the tasks we have to perform without the strength of God. The favor of the Lord is a continuing pattern in our lives when we become obedient to what God has called us to do.

The Lord is our teacher of all things in Christ; the spiritual ability we have and should use according to the measure of faith exists within us. God does not give us any ability to handle things that are not associated with Him. We are spiritual giants when it is associated with the spiritual things of God. We were mere people of small statues, but when we were born again, our minds and soul bonded with God. Now, we can use the strength of God. We are full of power to survive and not fail. The power of God is what we all need to run on. We are in a race when we join forces with God. We need to be ready to do the spiritual things of God; the spiritual strength is there for the asking. We will never be without it. It becomes our support: "We can do all things through Christ, which strengthens us."

Chapter Twenty

Special Anointing

To come before the Father in the pureness of a clean heart and soul, you first have to be washed in the blood of Jesus. The blood is the cleansing agent that will flow from Calvary to your home; the Father is the giver. The pureness of God comes from being obedient to the call of discipleship. The Father will be able to use you as a clean vessel whenever the call has been put upon your life; the call is important, and the temple is important. It will help you understand what you have to do to answer the special call of obedience. There will be some that will never come to this level in life because of the special life that one has to follow; the obedience of one is not what anyone can follow and be able to continue to follow. It is not hard; it is just the patience and obedience of one who has the time to work with the Father. God is true to their life, and they are true to God. The combination is awesome, and God will always honor the relationship. Moses and Abraham had this awesome relationship with the master; it is the supernatural call of God, and only a few have been able to supersede this call.

Out of love, you can look into the mysteries of God, and miracles will flow through your ministries by the will of the Father. Ask, and you will see what I am speaking to you about; walking with the Father down this road, you will open doors that many have passed by. You have to have a key that only God can and will give a very few of His children. I want to please the Father; whatever there is for me to have, let His will be done in my life. The road is tough; it belongs to the elect. There is power in the gift of God. God is offering it to you for the price of being pure and faithful to the Father. The gift is something that will help your ministries that will not be accomplished through everyone. Seek and pray and receive the gift of God; many will not be able to even know of this gift, a special gift of God, a pure gift for pure people.

Your responsibility is to honor and love God with all your heart and soul, and you will receive the things that most of the saints would be happy to possess. This is the awesome supernatural power of God. Get ready and stay that way so we can be filled with the power of God flowing from Calvary to home. I want this power of obedience in my life; I have offered myself to God forever and ever. I won't have to show anyone what it is; it will be visible in everything that happens in my ministry. There are trials that one will have to be able to go through, and you can do it; it has been proven before. This is not too hard to conquer; the gift is worth the trials. I thank God for giving me whatever He wants me to possess to help my soul-saving ministry for the master.

I ask you, Father, to use me for my call. The call is wonderful, and my obedience has won the attention of God: "a few men in the army of the Lord." What an awesome call the Father will give just for loving and following Him. Get cleaned up with the blood and stay that way so that God can use you, too!

Everyone will want what you have, you will stand before your brothers and sisters, and the glow will illuminate you like it did Moses when he came off of Mt Horeb when God chose him to become the leader of the children of Israel. Moses was ready to answer this call and was able to stand before God with a pure heart and a willing mind to please God. Each of us should have the same willingness, but some will not make it because of the severity of the call. I don't know how to explain this; you have to come before God and be tested with the trials of life and let the Holy Spirit become your protector and guide, and you will overcome and be chosen by God. It is tough, but only the strong survive for the special call of God. Oh, how wonderful it is to walk in the presence of God, holding hands with the righteousness of God. All the angels in heaven will rejoice when you are chosen for this job; the demons in hell will also know when you are chosen, but God will protect you for the special job of God. This is special to you and God.

Doors that have never opened to you before will be open to you; doors that have opened to you that you had no need of entering will close to you. The protection of God will be yours until the harvest comes in. "Praise God! This is the work of God; this job is one that we cannot perform without a relationship with the Spirit of God. Now I see what Benny Hinn speaks about, Oral Roberts, and others. Not many can speak about this gift; it is the supernatural ability of God. No one knows who will be chosen; it is a gift that only God gives; it comes from the heart, a place you cannot disguise. The true love of God flows from the small place that sits in the protected part of our body. Now I know what Isaiah 40:31 is expressing: *"But they that wait upon the Lord shall renew their strength; they shall mount up with wings as eagles; they shall run, and not be weary; and they shall walk, and not faint."* "For the special anointing of God"

Our Spiritual Motivation

We should be motivated to be more pleasing to God and to show ourselves approved unto God (2 Timothy 2:15) as children ready to do God's will at all cost. We, as children of God, are a tool to be used for the glory of God, so let our light shine so that there is no darkness in the world or us. We, as Christians, are chosen to finish the work God has given each and every one of us to complete. Therefore, God said that no weapon formed against us shall prosper because of the protection that the Father has given us so that there is no concern for us to be worried about the enemy attack, but go ahead and bring in the harvest for God.

There will be times that we will be sluggish, but this is not a time of relaxation but a time of work. There are fields of people who are ready to answer the call of God but do not know what to say or do. If we only provide them the way, the harvest will be plenty, and we will reap a profit for God, and all our joy will be fulfilled in gathering the sheep for God. Let us all get ready and go out to gather what we have been called to do. There is joy in the morning, and there is peace along the way. Come on, children of God, let us finish what Christ came to earth to finish. It is up to us to bring in the sheep; that is what this is all about, so that we will be pleasing in God's sight and not in the sight of men.

We are children of light, so get your lantern and keep it filled so that your light will continue to glow so that no one here on earth will be lost and cannot find the way to the Father. That is why God has called us so that we will be the world's light to the lost. Come on and get to work and stay that way until the job is completed, and make our Father proud to have called us to join forces against the enemy and come out victorious. We are not just stewards of the word; we are doers. Increase your territory and let the blood of Jesus flow through the lives of many.

"Let us all come on and go into what God has called us for with a pure heart and a willing mind and be a winner for God and a loser for the enemy."

Chapter Twenty-one

What a Friend We Have In Jesus

The dead in Christ will rise first. Those standing will be caught up in the air with the Lord. On that great and glorious day! Our Lord returns to get his church. We, the body of Christ, should be ready, for no one knows when our Savior will return; it will be quick and soon. No one will be left behind if you stay prepared, pray, be ready, and stay that way. Will you be counted when that great and glorious day comes? Will you be counted when Jesus returns to get His church? Will you be asleep? Or will you be awake? The day is coming, and the time will approach for us all that will be ready when our savior will return. Get ready, saints of God, you know the plans, you know what was said. Don't be left in the dark; stay in the light; there is a reward for each and every one of us.

The end is here; you and I know, without a doubt, we will be leaving soon. Only the ones that believe will be going home. 'Without faith, it is impossible to please God.' Get your faith hat on and make sure it fits; you don't want it to fall off; hold onto what you have. That is what will assure us of a safe passage home.

Don't just look gazing into the sky; it will be sudden. Just watch and see. It will be glorious for you and me. Count your blessing if you are counted in His glorious return that had won victory over the wiles of the devil.

Victory, victory, what a wonderful sound; I love to hear that word. I know we, as Christians, have won the battle that has been fought for so long. The reward is here, and the time to count our blessings is here. Patience is the key to our salvation, and now look at what a reward we have to receive. I know, without a doubt, the victory will be sweet, the ride will be smooth, we will all go to meet the Lord, and He will take us home. "Oh, how long have we waited for this to come to pass? Now look at our reward. God is a great and wonderful provider and lies never enter his mouth. He said we would receive it if only we would believe; now it is here without a doubt.

The price of life is the way we live our lives; now look, the pay is here. The blood was flowing, and look at what it did for you and me. The cross is too far away for us to touch, but the blood will flow and free us all. *(2corinthian 5:7)* says, *for we walk by faith and not by sight.* Those who believe will see for themselves that there is a God that will provide for them. The children of God are the father's most proud possession. He will give them their heart's desire if only they will believe and faint not. Faith is for those who will run this course and faint not. To believe is one of the most wonderful things we can have to achieve the grandest prize the father has for us; it is the prize of life. Faith is the key that will open all the doors to our ministries and all that God has for us. Faith is possible if only we believe. Faith is faith, and it cannot be replaced. Faith is what will move God to act on our behalf and do the impossible in our lives. If there is a mountain that has to be removed, faith will crush it into powder, and it will be no more; if there is a valley, it will be wiped out as if it has never existed. Faith is a precious commodity in our lives. It is what we, as Christians, need and to keep.

The more we believe, the more we will receive. Faith is what a friend we have in Jesus, the solution to everything. It is the key to all the mysteries of God; we will enter the things of God that have not been revealed to many because they are the deep things of God that no one will be able to unlock. It is a supernatural possession of the one who is supernatural. Faith is the reason we breathe and can possess the things of God. We cannot and will not receive without it.

Walking and talking to God is a faith mission; without it, you cannot and will not survive. Faith is the Elshaddai of our being. Oh, how faith will move mountains. It starts small, but when you activate it, it becomes as large as you desire, and it has been told that it will become the power that explodes into our lives, and we will never know where it will lead us; only God knows. Keep walking by faith and not by sight, and you will see what I am speaking about.

Faith is like an atomic bomb that has the power to move over the distance of the earth; Faith is more powerful than that. It can disseminate and go into many people's hearts and minds to plant a seed to grow into more than we can even think or know. Faith is the growth of life that God gives us, the measure of faith. It's up to each and every one of us to water or let it become stagnant in our lives. Faith is that power of possession, our most proud possession if only we will believe. Take your share of faith and get in touch with God and the provision that he has provided, and you will see the impossible that will grow into your life; it is the seed of life. It is the growth we need, and you can be sure we will not survive without it.

When you come to God, you must believe, or you will not be able to receive or possess God's things in your life. Your faith can be what you or I develop it into. Hold onto your faith, whether it is a tiny seed or whatever; it is better to have some faith than not any at all. We all are not going to be able to develop our faith at the same rate, but we can be sure we will have the measure of faith that God has given each and every one of us. Now, what we do with it is up to us; as a way of speaking, the monkey is on your back; you can wear it or cast it aside. You are in a position to make a decision without the help of God, and this is your choice. Faith is the motor in your life; you can keep it going or just leave it without giving it the maintenance it needs and let it become un-operative, where it will become impossible to move. Keep your faith polished and growing, and you will see what I am speaking of. I don't have to prove to you, but faith will. Faith is the impossible to each and every one of us that will believe. Amen!

Hebrews 11:1&6 says, *"Now faith is the substance of things hoped for, the evidence of things not seen (v6) But without faith it is impossible to please him: for he that cometh to God must believe that he is a rewarder of them that diligently seek him.*

Chapter Twenty-Two

Lyric of God

Here am I send me Lord!

The battle is hot, the war is long, the time is short, where will I go? "O Lord, where will I go? There is a season I know, and there is a season I see. The time is here to follow thee. Where will I go? O Lord, where will I go, send me. O Lord, send me. I am here for your call; send me. I am here. O Lord, send me. Where will I go? "O Lord, where will I go? Your time is precious. O Lord, your time is not free; send me. O Lord, send me. The hour has come. I am willing to go; send me. The days are here; the battle is near. Send me. I want to see your smile. O Lord, send me. What will I do? O Lord, send me. Your presence is sweet; your voice is near. O Lord, please send me. Where can I find you, Lord? Where will you be? I am coming to you. O Lord, I am coming to you. Let me see the way to you; let me see the way. I am here for the call; I am here for the call. Where will I go? O Lord, where will I go? Send me. The hour is here; the time is near. Send me. I am here for your call. Oh Lord, send me.

Where will I go? O Lord, where will I go? I hear you, master. I hear your call. I am ready for the call; please send me."

"Victory is here for the joy of the Lord; victory is here for me too. Send me, O Lord, send me. O, how wonderful are you calling. I am ready to surrender to your call. Sweetly are you calling, please send me. O Lord, please, please send me. What are you saying? O Lord, I hear your call; send me. O Lord, send me. Victory is your call. I know, without a doubt, you are calling me. I know, Lord, you are calling me. Sweetly are you calling me, and sweetly do I hear your call. O Lord, sweetly do I hear your call. The job is now. I know, without a doubt, I need to come to you. How can I count the time of your call? How can I be called? O Lord, how long will you call me? O Lord, how long will you call me?"

"The wind is blowing; I hear your call. How can I come to you? Sweetly, are you calling. How can I come to you? Father of fathers, your mercy is here for you and me; your mercy is here for the call, O Lord. Where will you be? I am here for the call. Use me for the day, which is here; use me for your call."

Chapter Twenty-three

My wilderness Walk

"While I was walking in the wilderness, what I am speaking of is a separation from habits that I once desired and was focusing only on the things of God. This was my wilderness. The grace of God was upon my life. Without God, I would not have triumphed through the trials I went through; the journey was an experience, and I would not advise anyone to travel without the approval of God. When the journey is all and final, you can say you have received strength that had been hidden in your inner being. The journey is rewarding, but there is a price. Walking with Jesus is the most rewarding part of it. You don't have the congregation members to call upon when the journey becomes unbearable. You hold up both hands; sometimes, this is a sign of surrender unto God; you pray and cry out, asking God for strength that He can give. There are times you will want to turn around, but what are you turning around to? Where you left was a wilderness that had no final reward but the destruction of the body and soul. With God, I could have a positive outcome from following Him; I would receive a reward of life. My wilderness walk has been very educational; my teacher is the Holy Spirit. We became bonded; my thoughts were to keep Him happy, and I knew that pleases Him. He would continue to guide, comfort, and teach me.

The walk of faith is what this is, and God is the one who orchestrates it all. I was washed and cleansed with the word; I went through the fire and was cured for the job. I needed the anointing for the ministry. Without the purifying, I could not be equipped for the final call on my life. The travel constitutes many lumpy roads, with some smooth places. There were hills and valleys with seemingly no ends. Feeling lost and deserted, but within my inner being, I knew that God would not leave me nor forsake me (Joshua 1:5). Sometimes it was hard to remember those words. The flesh would creep in and say, "Enough is enough. Haven't you done what God has called you to do? Where is the reward? I don't see one." I would say to myself, "Go back to where you were and see if it will be the same." I knew within my heart that I didn't want the carousel of death; it was like playing Russian roulette, not knowing if the next pull would be the last.

Each time my strength became weak, my Heavenly Father would send in a spiritual ration that my soul clearly needed if I were to go all the way through in my right mind. There were times

I wanted to say, "Lord, I don't want the job; let me be a regular person sitting in the pews on Sundays. I know He would smile at me and say, "It's too late; you have joined the army of the Lord; it is too late to turn around." The Father would say, "Keep it up; you are doing well; your enlistment is getting ready to pay off, and you will be greatly rewarded." That was good to hear for a while, but until there was another valley or a higher mountain, I didn't know if I should crawl or walk. If it was not for the Holy Spirit, which was a great support, I knew, without a doubt, I would not have made it through.

A calling on your life is not a birthday party with cake and ice cream; it is something different that each one of us has a story to tell of our own. I do believe that when you are called, you experience different degrees of anointing upon your life. The stronger your faith, the more fire of cleansing is put upon you with more responsibilities.

My wilderness walk was educational; as I stated earlier, God prepares your body and mind to be ready for the job. Wisdom, knowledge, and understanding of God's words develops that you had no idea it was stored in your brain. You open your mouth and God has a new revelation that comes out. Your spiritual life develops like a butterfly that comes out of a cocoon. You begin to think like God and want what God wants and do it. Your life will be centered on Him and the things of God.

When the words of God begin to manifest, you see the mystery in them. That seems to jump out and say here is what God is saying. You begin to get that rush of excitement that you can't get enough of. You will spend hours studying, seeking to see what mystery is going to be revealed today. You feel like God has chosen you, and no one else seems important. That's not true; in reality, He does that to anyone who truly surrenders to His call. I would constantly thank God for taking the time and giving me the opportunity to be used for a special call into the ministry. He has a choice to choose whom He desires, but this time, it was me. Hallelujah!

For years in my life, I felt like I had failed, but now I see God was preparing me to step out of my cocoon and become this beautiful, educated butterfly with the word of God to teach, build, and be a blessing in His kingdom. What a reward to receive. I glance back at the beginning of my walk and see why it was important for my ten-year journey through the valley, feeling alone. It was not to destroy me but to rid myself of the old man so that the new man in Christ may surface and perform a job God intended for each and every one of us that will surrender and will be able to enjoy laboring in the kingdom of God.

Only the strong survive

When you go through something and come out of it, you should be teachable, depending only on the Father and not the flesh. Without trials being broken down, you will stay in self, and God will not be able to reach you to receive the anointing of God. A wilderness walk is a new birth, so God can mold you the way He wants you. My brain was working overtime to hear what God wanted me to accomplish, not Alice! They become bonds that cannot be broken. The dependency on God is all He wants from each and every one of us. Some of us are very hard to mold, and some are very willing to go through what God has for us to walk through the valley holding hands with God the Almighty. I was one of the very hard ones to mold.

It really turned out to be a wonderful, refreshing trip with many adventures that sometimes were unexplainable. Sometimes, the wilderness has nutrients that our mind and body need to understand the concept God has for us. Without it, our dependency is elsewhere, and our minds will not be ready to conceive. This is a power walk with God. You receive the anointing of God to supersede the ability you had before to conquer what you have been called to do. The ability we began with cannot submit to what God has called us to perform. The first obstacle you face will seem like a giant, and if you're unprepared, you will turn and run back where you started. We need to go forward, go through whatever situation there may be, and the giant that we once were afraid of going on to the next without spending time with the last.

With the anointing of God, you will be equipped to conquer whatever. We also received some portion of the same power that other disciples of God had put on their lives, depending on the strength that we, as individuals, can handle. The anointing of God is like armor; if you are not strong enough, the armor will weigh you down and drag you instead of holding you up and sending you into battle. When I finally reached the end of my journey, I was very excited to come out and go about my Father's business. I was sent back to church, ready and eager to mingle with the people of God. I wanted to complete what had loose ends and tidy up what was necessary. Whatever I was called to do, "here am I" (1 Samuel 3:4-8). As Samuel said, when God called him, he was a child ready for the battle. So was I; I had completed my training in the wilderness, and whatever God wanted me to tackle, I had no fear or regrets, willing to pursue whatever God had for me to the end. Thank God! It is finished: "The Wilderness Walk." I found peace and strength in the prayer; each day, I would say the Ephesians prayer. *"Ephesians 6:10-18; the whole armor of God. "Finally, my brethren, be strong in the Lord, and in the power of his might.*

Put on the whole armor of God that ye may be able to stand against the wiles of the devil. For we wrestle not against flesh and blood, but against principalities, against powers, against the rulers of the darkness of this world, against spiritual wickedness in high places. Wherefore take unto you the whole armor of God, that ye may be able to withstand in the evil day, and having done all, to stand, Stand therefore, having your loins girt about with truth, and having on the breastplate of righteousness; And your feet shod with the preparation of the gospel of peace; Above all, taking the shield of faith, wherewith ye shall be able to quench all the fiery darts of the wicked. And take the helmet of salvation, and the sword of the spirit, which is the word of God: Praying always with all prayer and supplication for all saints." Among many other scriptures, I clothe my mind with the things of God, Praying without ceasing. AMEN!

www.ingramcontent.com/pod-product-compliance
Lightning Source LLC
LaVergne TN
LVHW010557160826
845677LV00013B/3156

9798891210110